Enjoy !

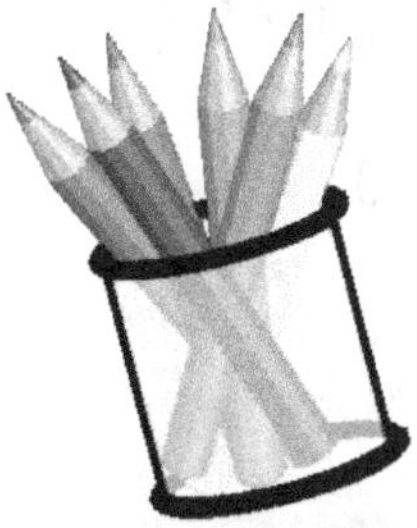

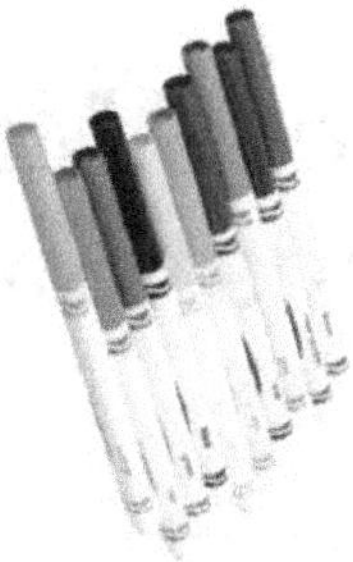

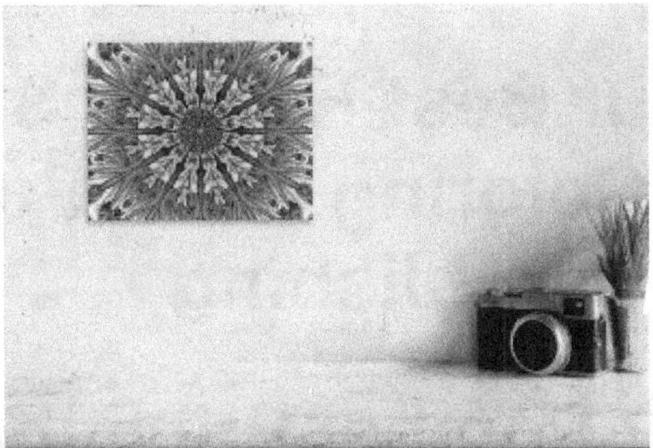

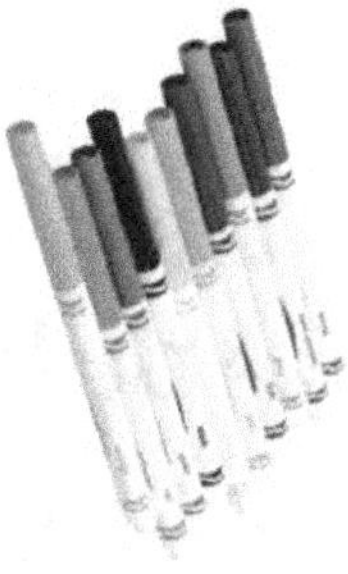

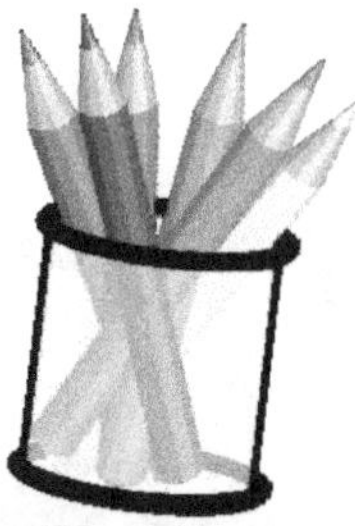

Be Your Best
Relieve Stress
Mandala
Adult Coloring Book

AUTHOR

Pompei Publishing

Be Your Best Relieve Stress Mandala
Adult Coloring Book Published by
Pompei Publishing

© 2019 Pompei Publishing

Cover by Pompei Publishing

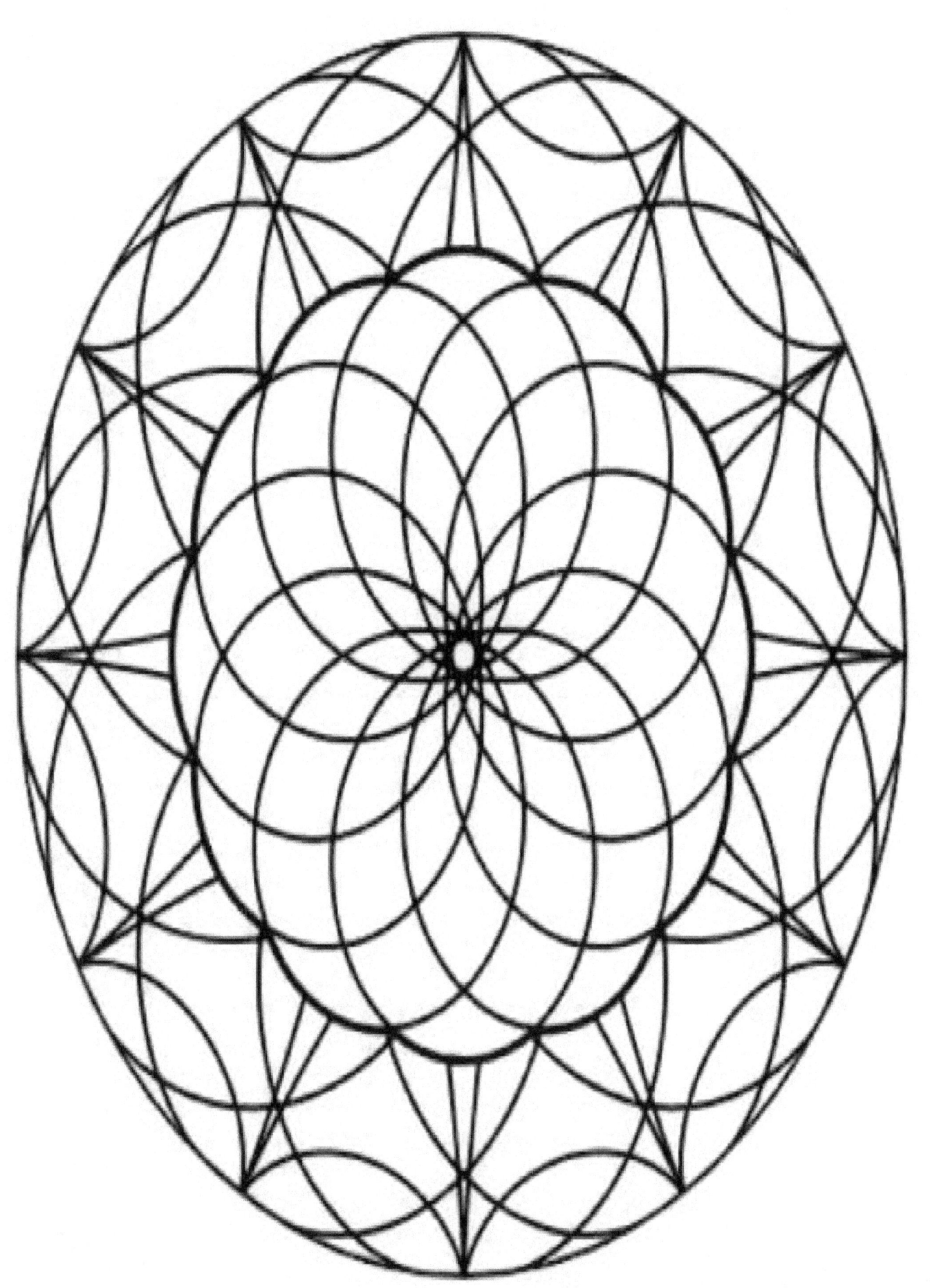

BLANK

PAGE

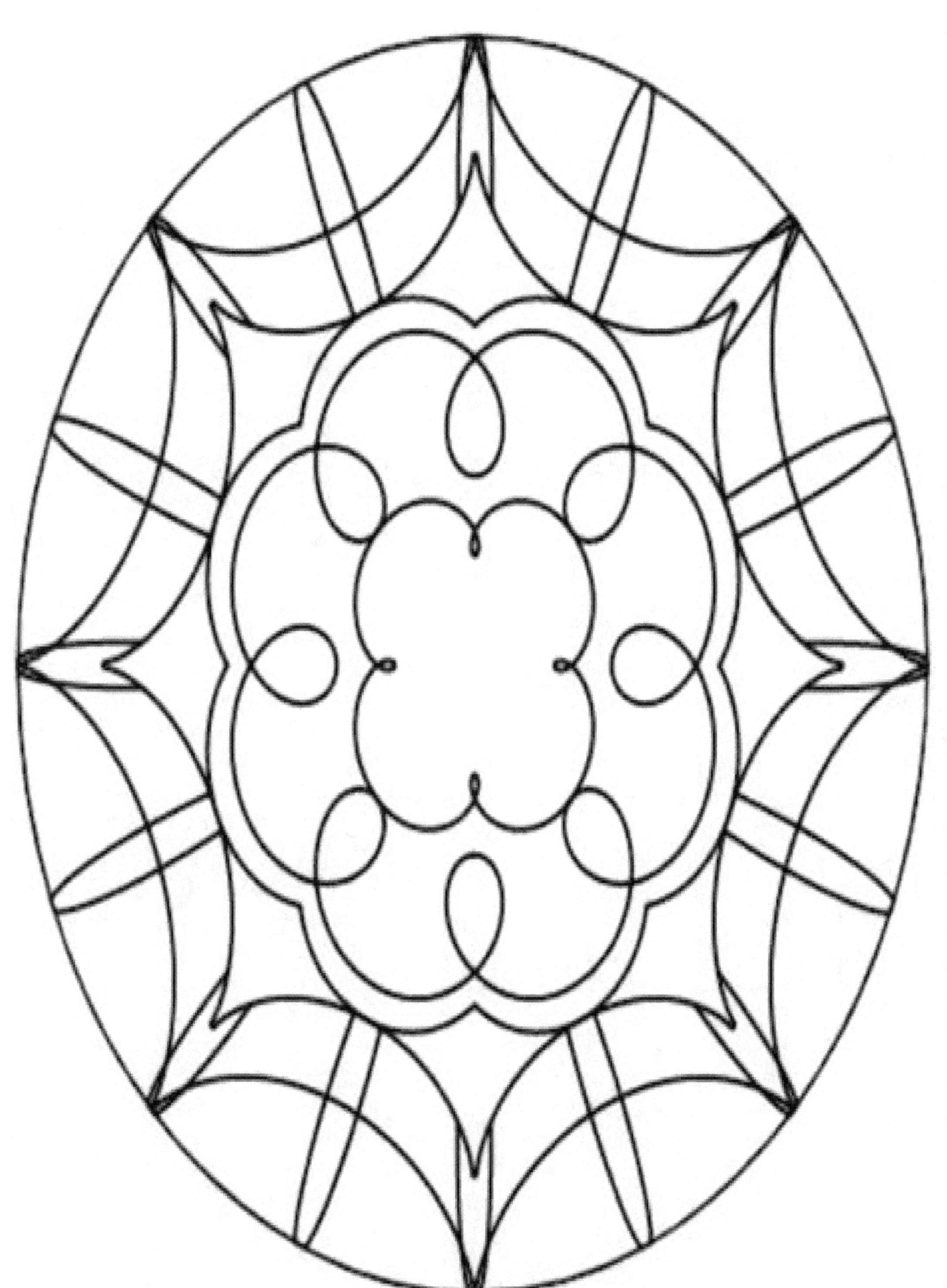

BLANK

PAGE

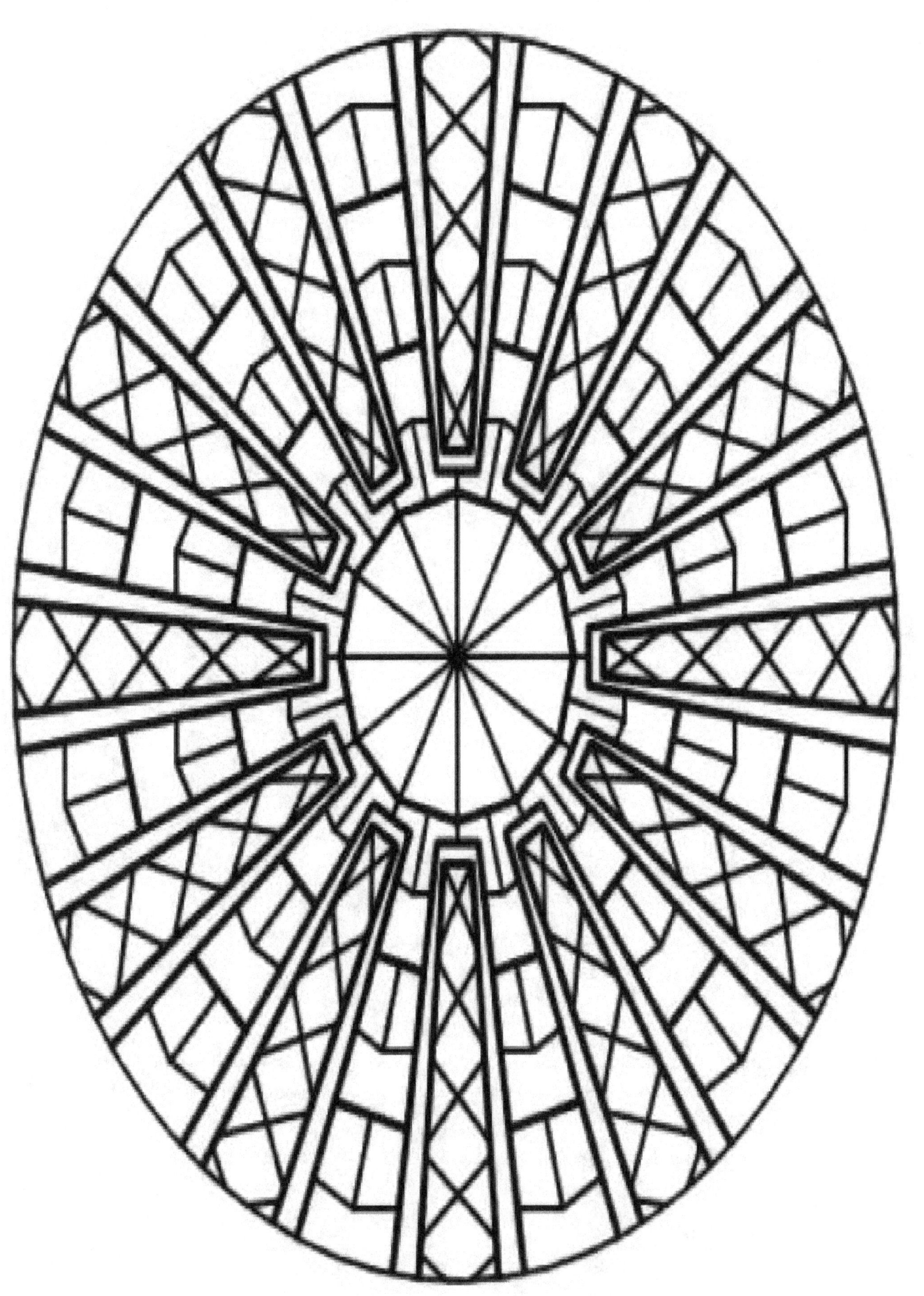

BLANK

PAGE

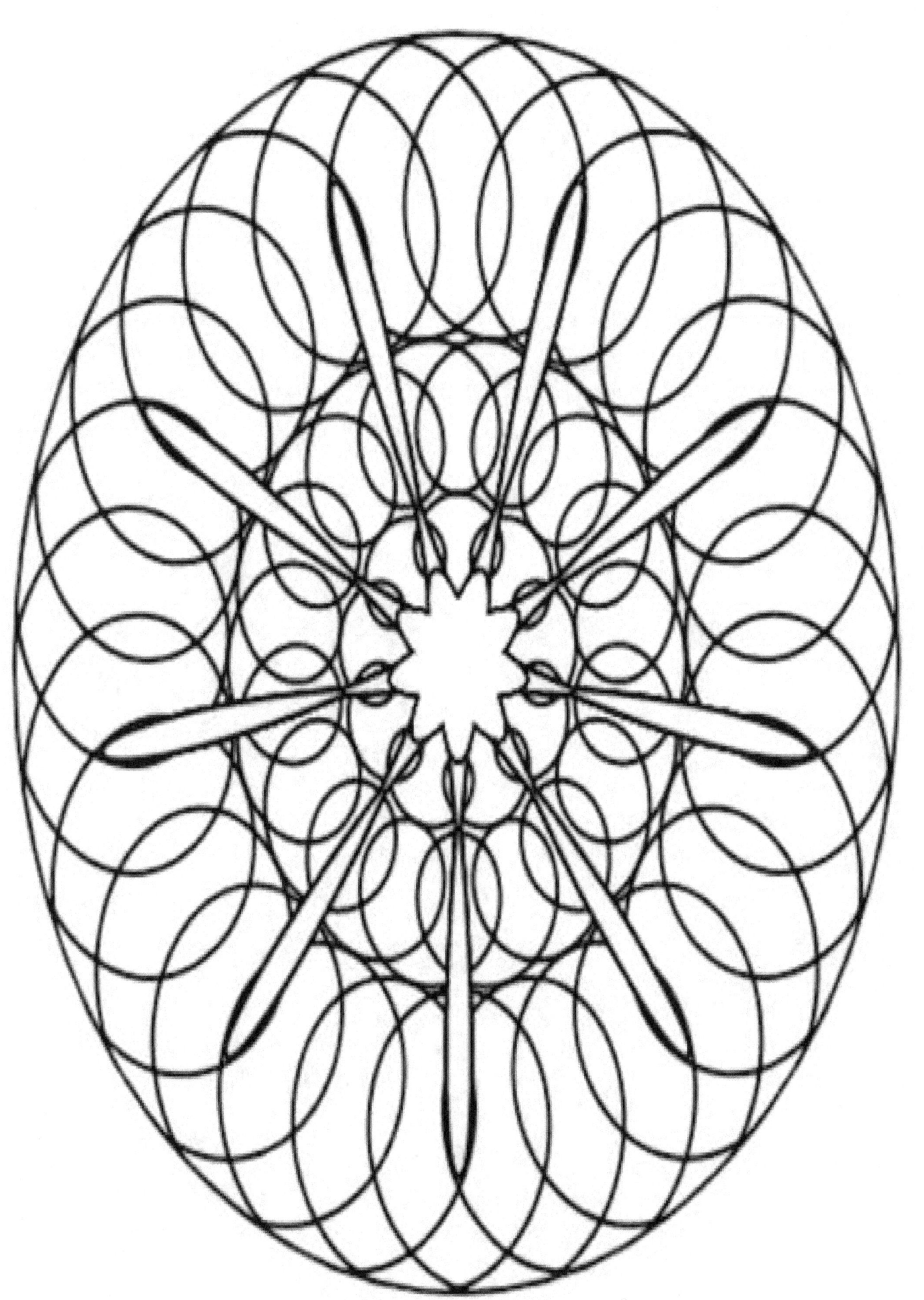

BLANK

PAGE

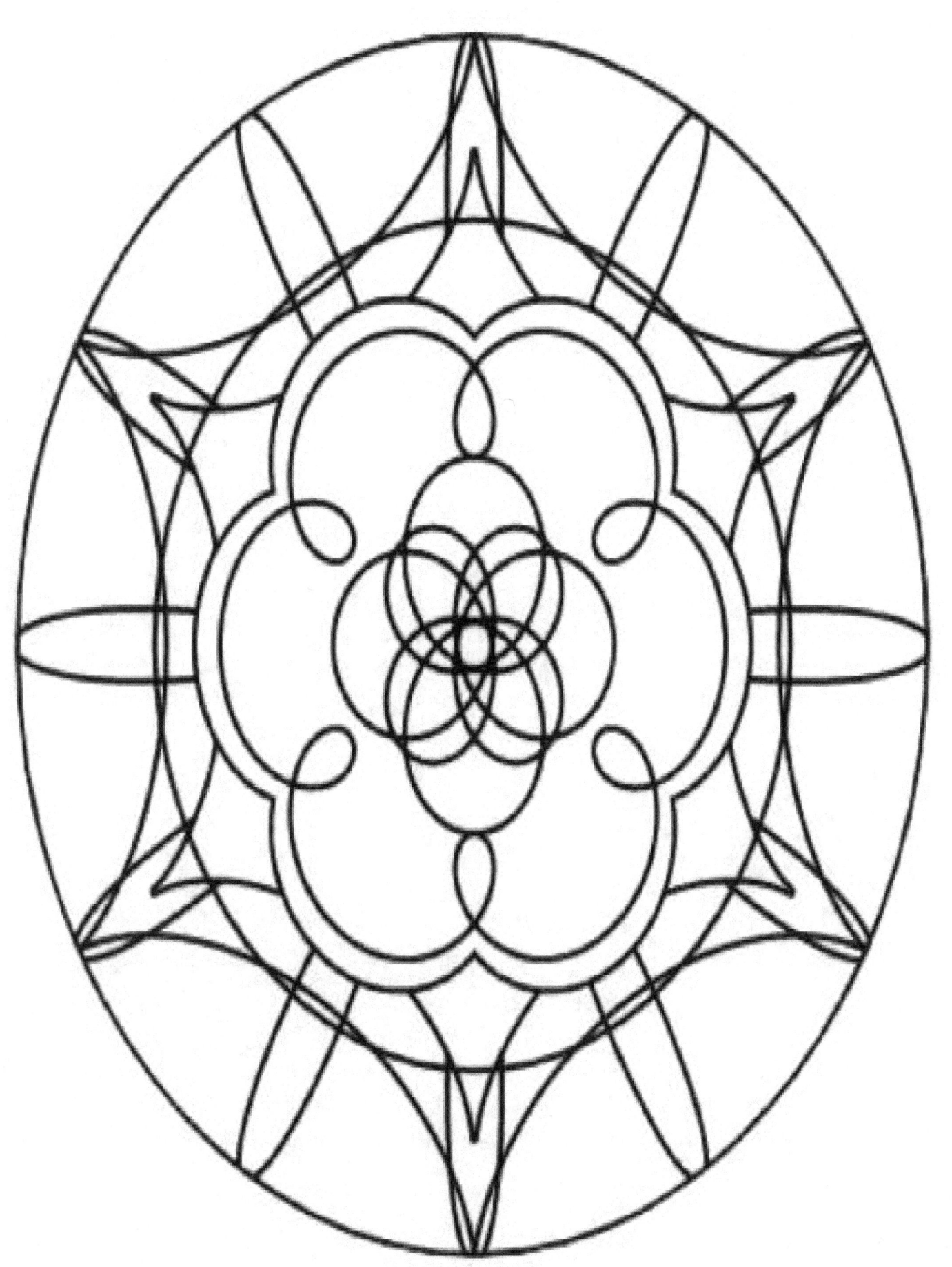

BLANK

PAGE

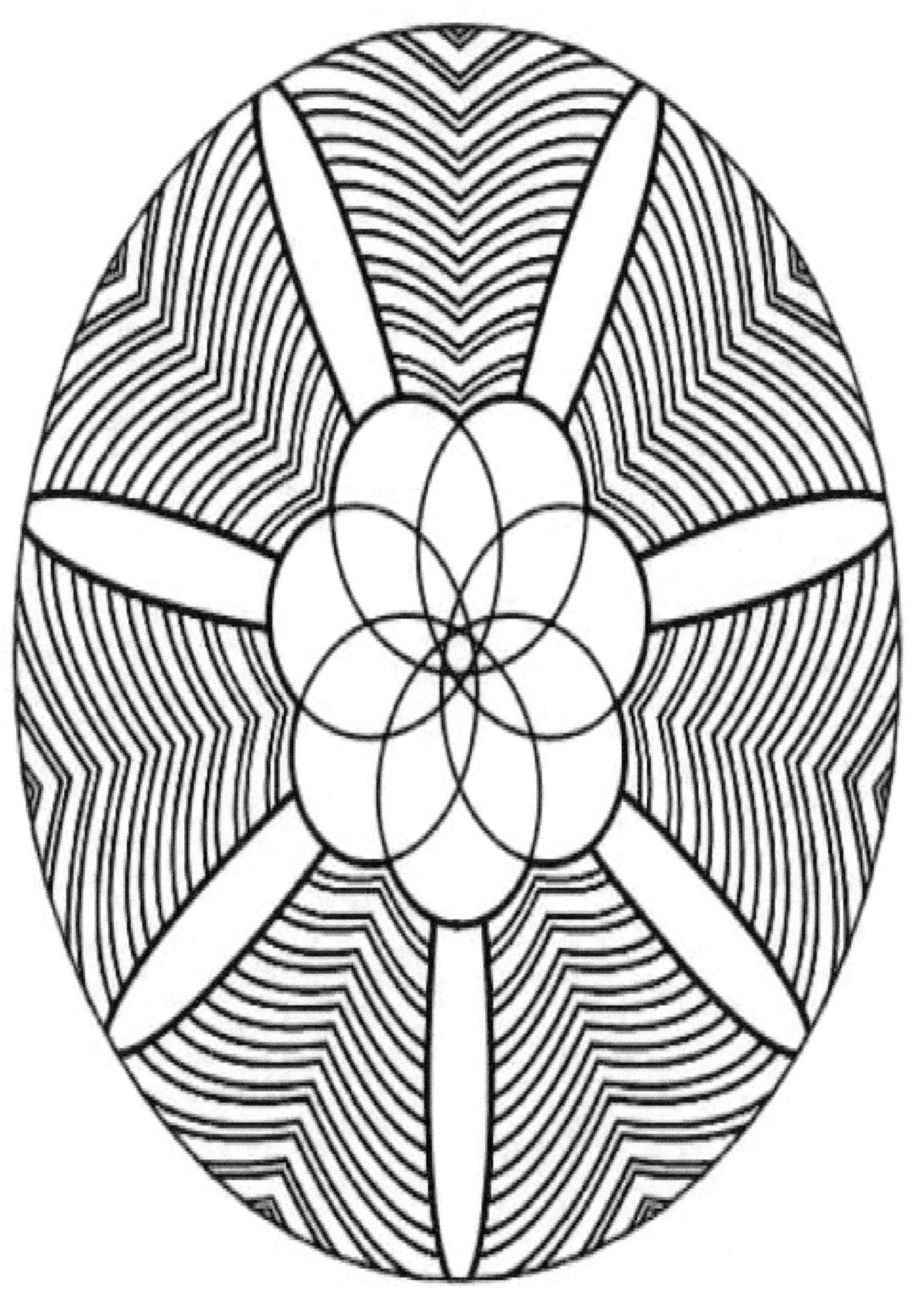

BLANK

PAGE

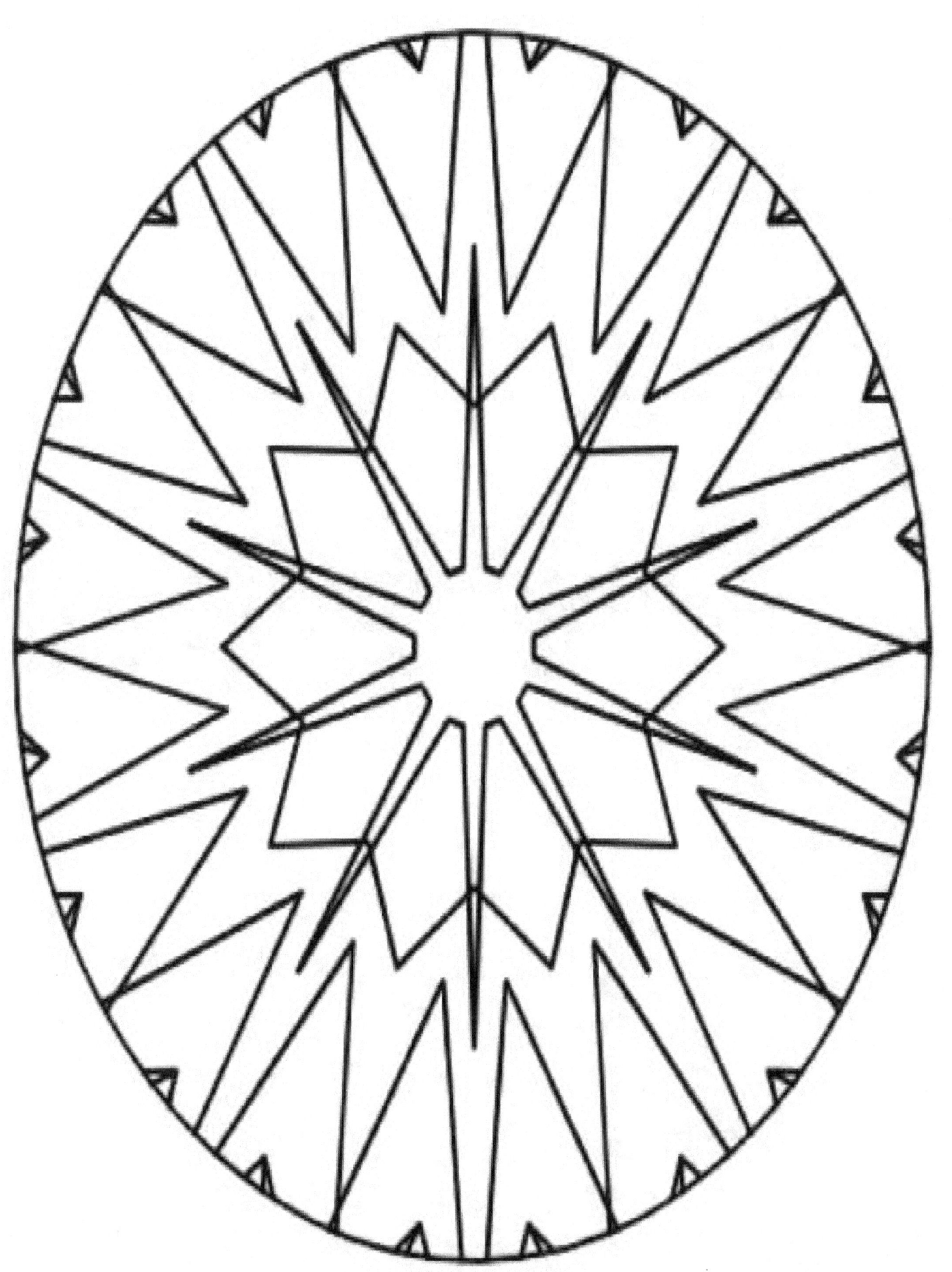

BLANK

PAGE

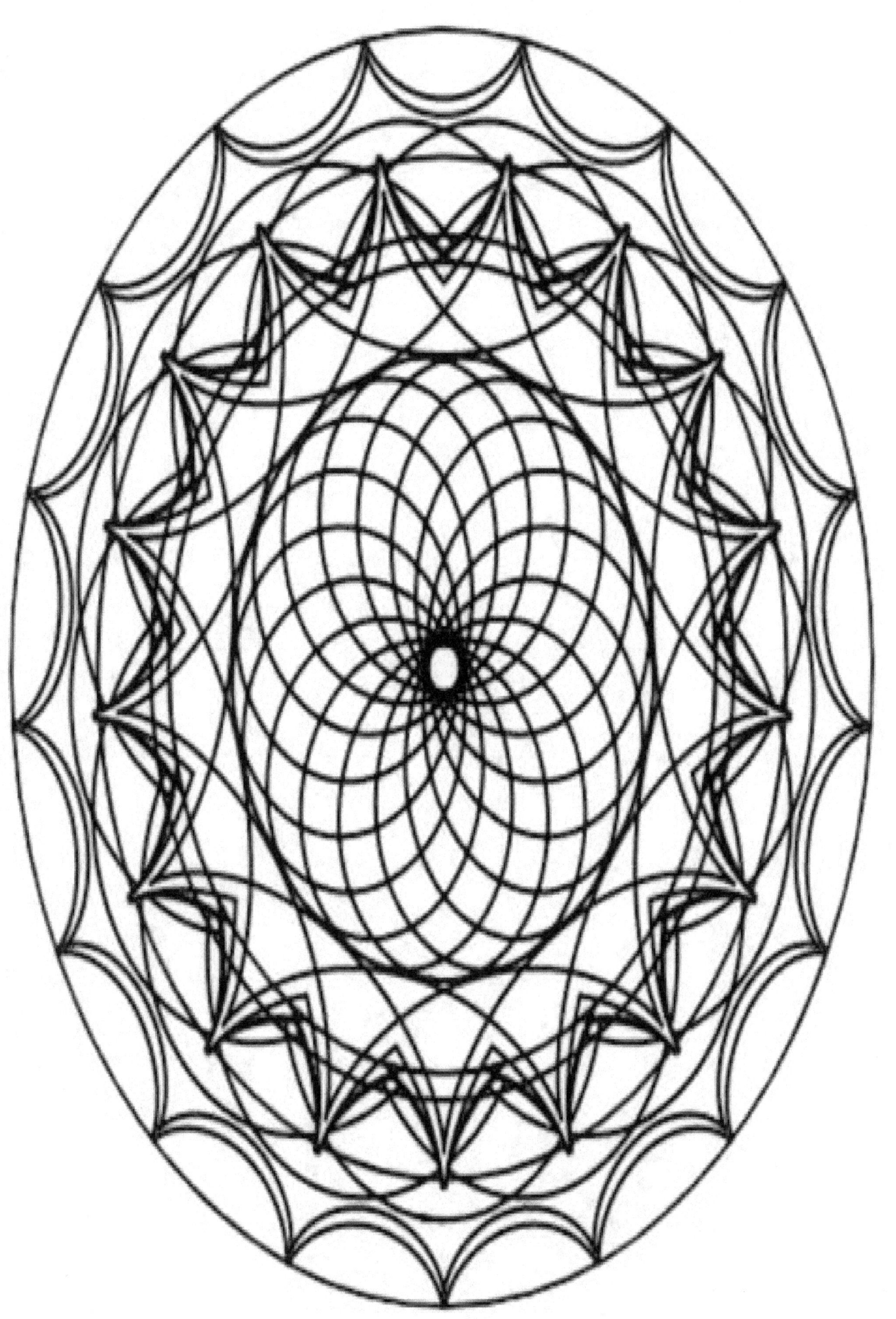

BLANK PAGE

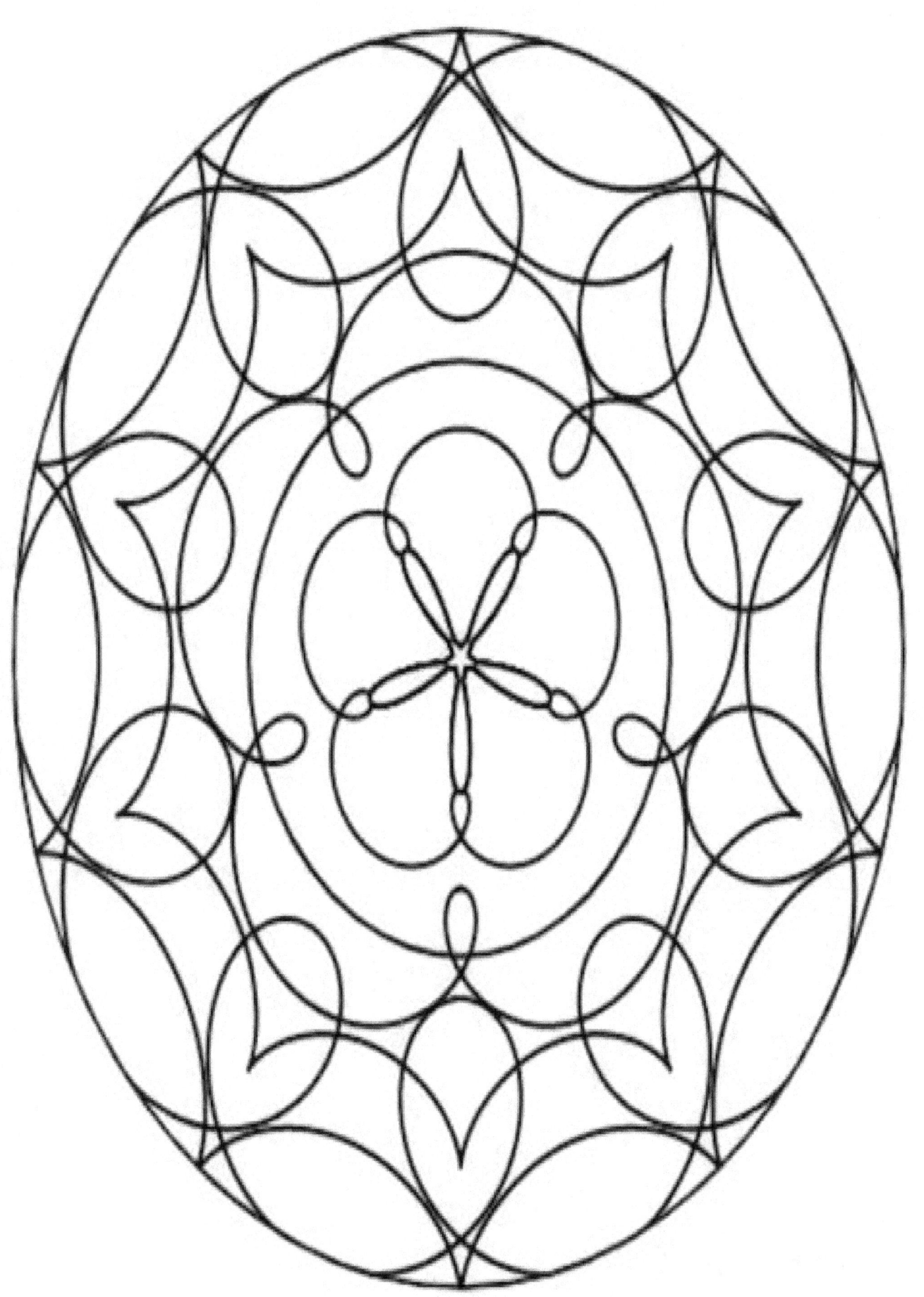

BLANK

PAGE

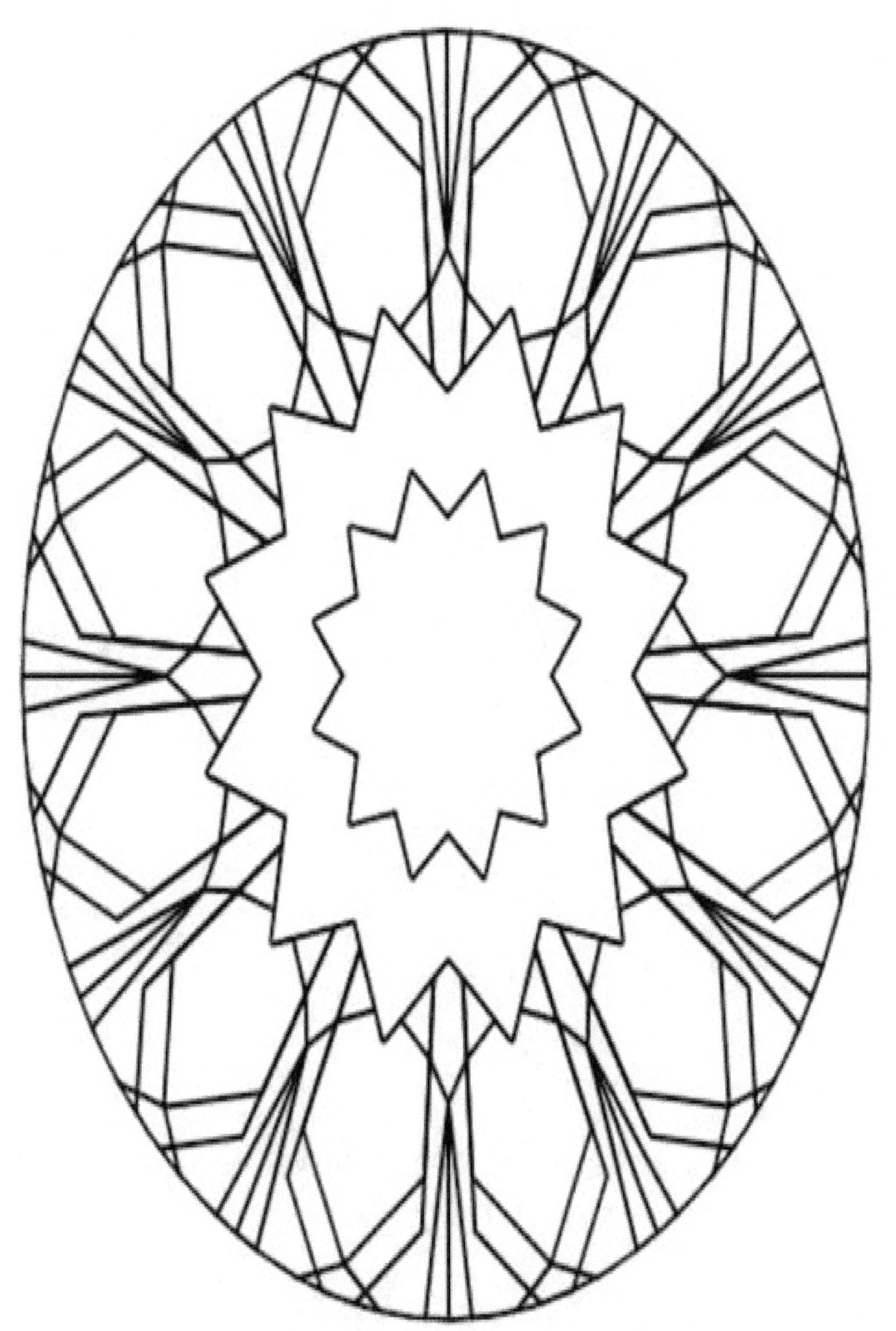

BLANK

PAGE

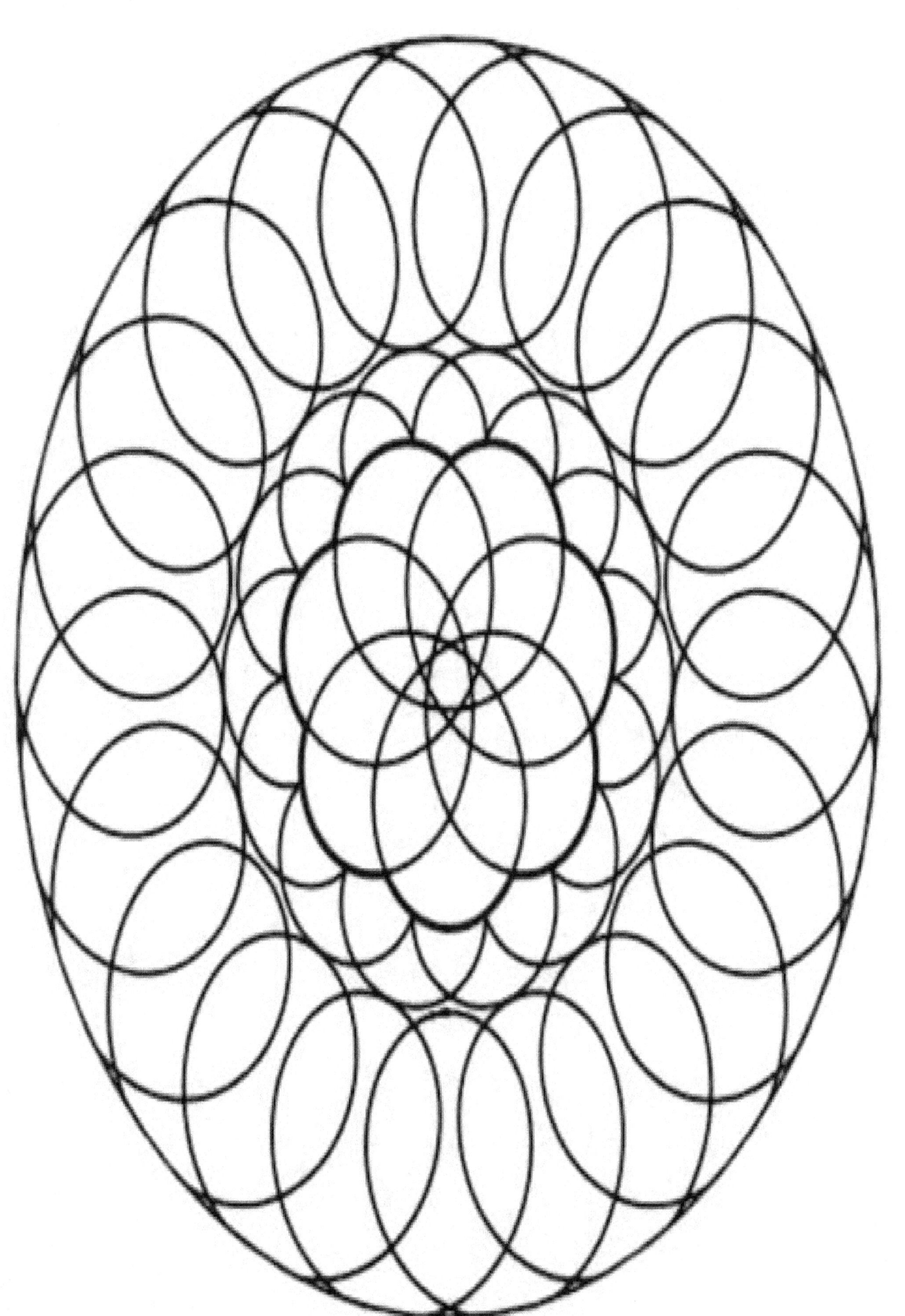

BLANK

PAGE

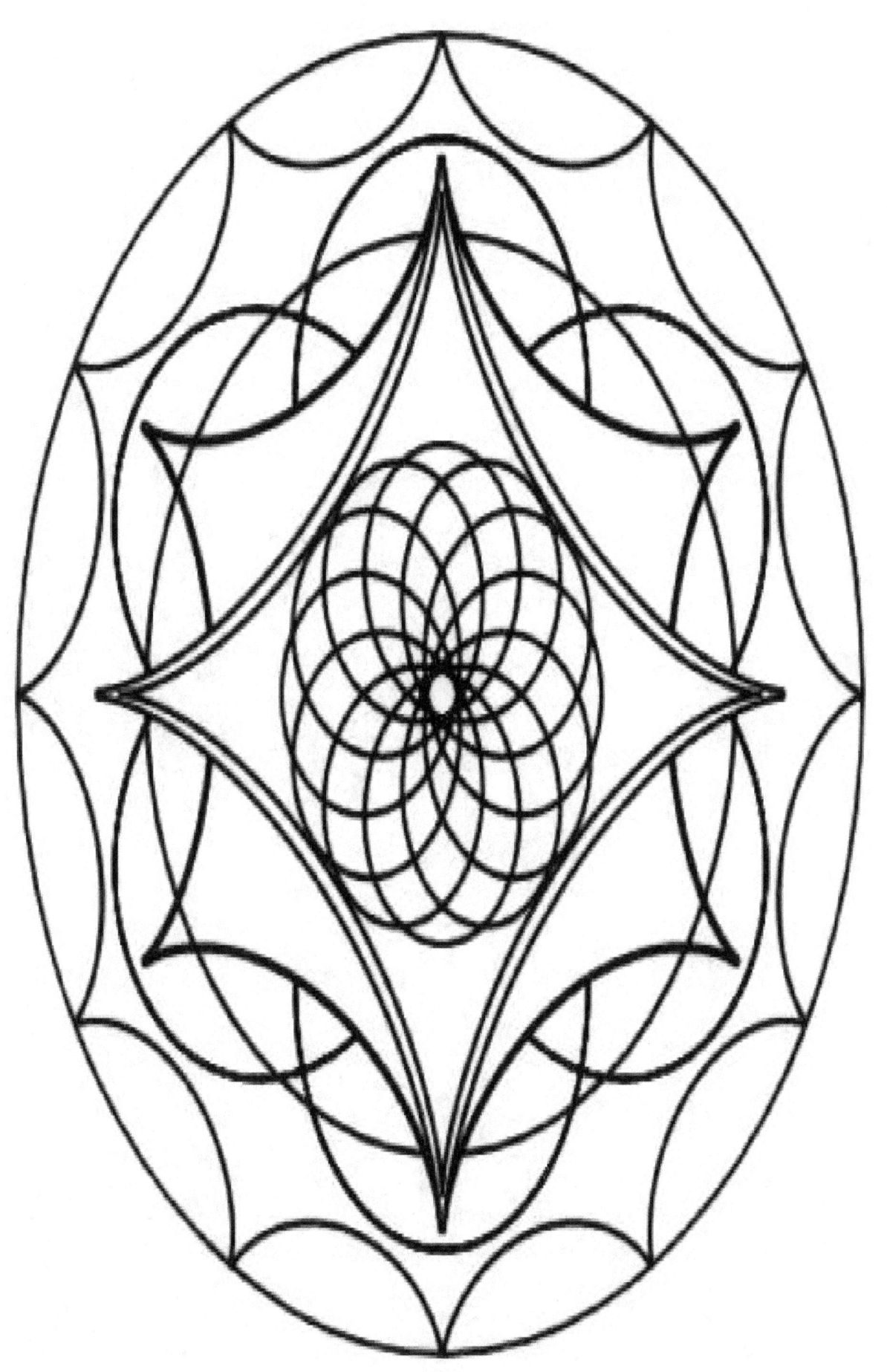

BLANK

PAGE

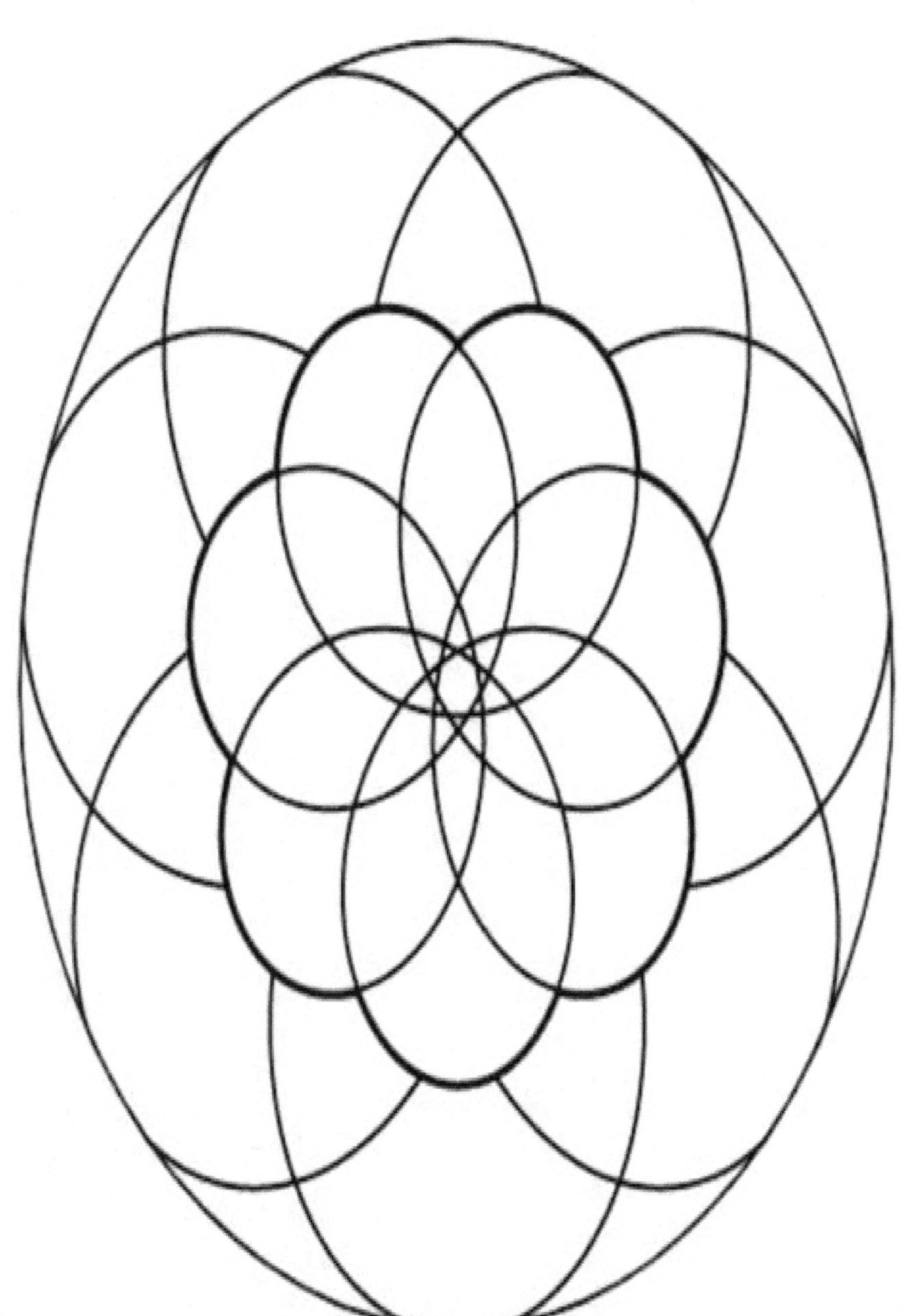

BLANK

PAGE

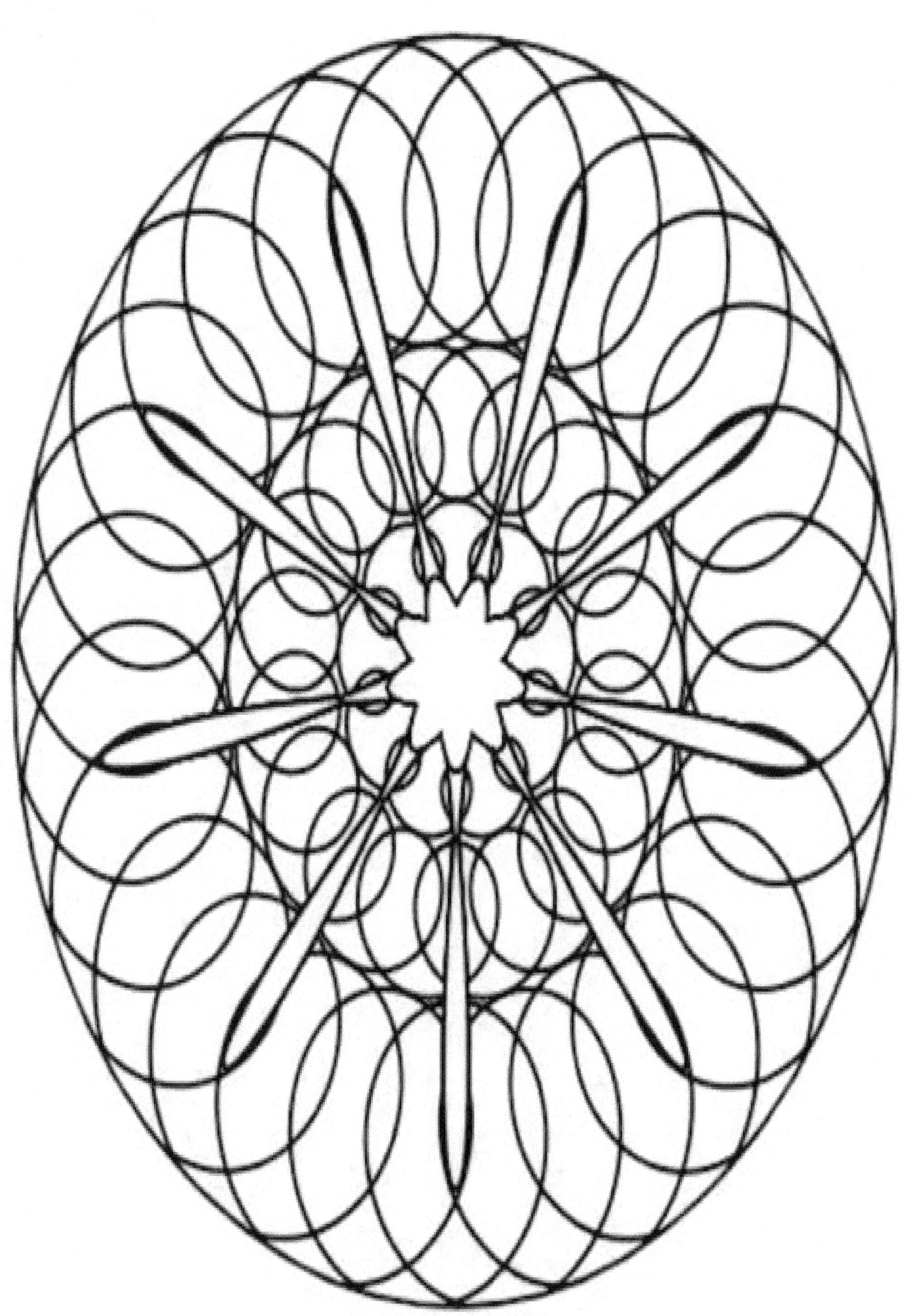

BLANK

PAGE

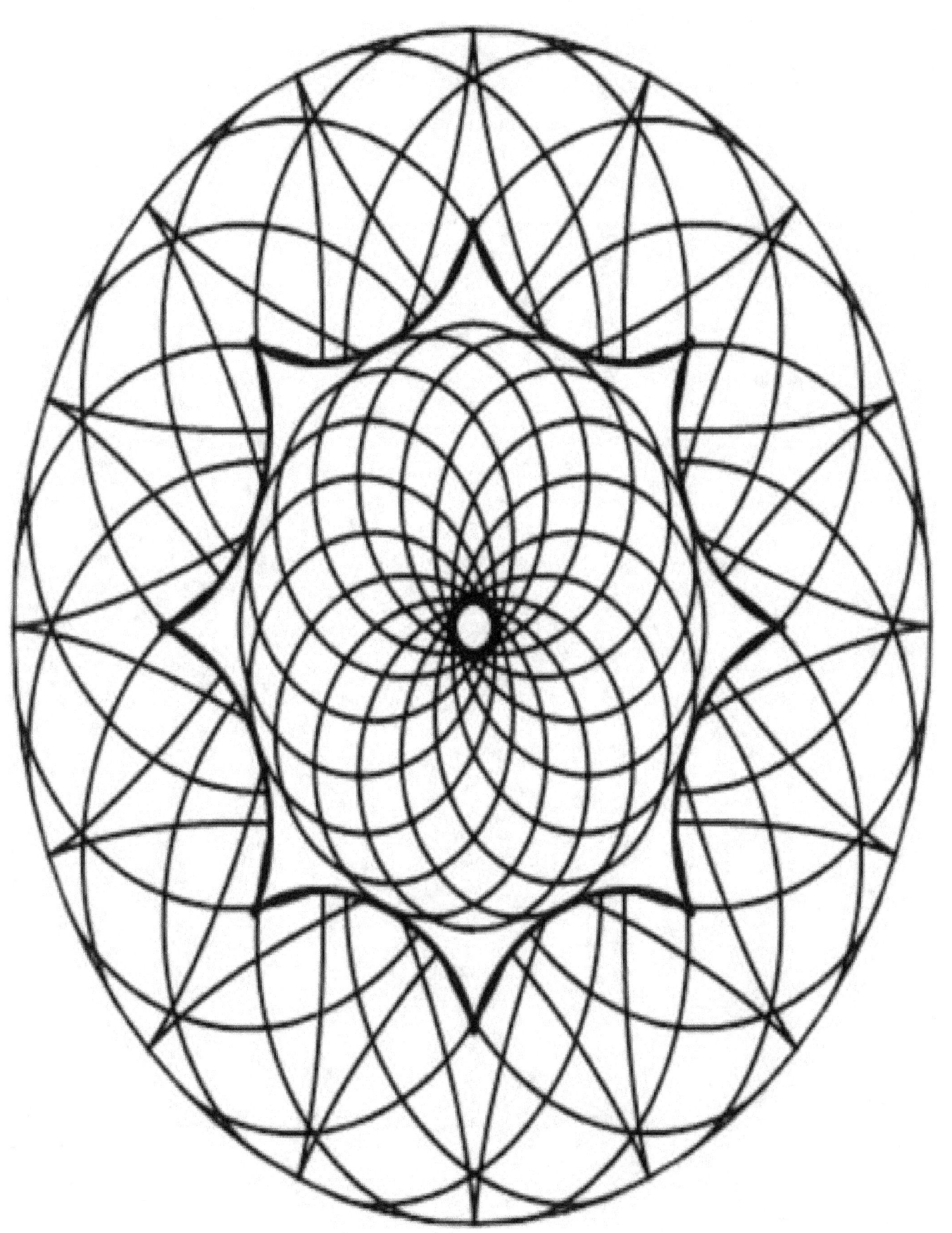

BLANK

PAGE

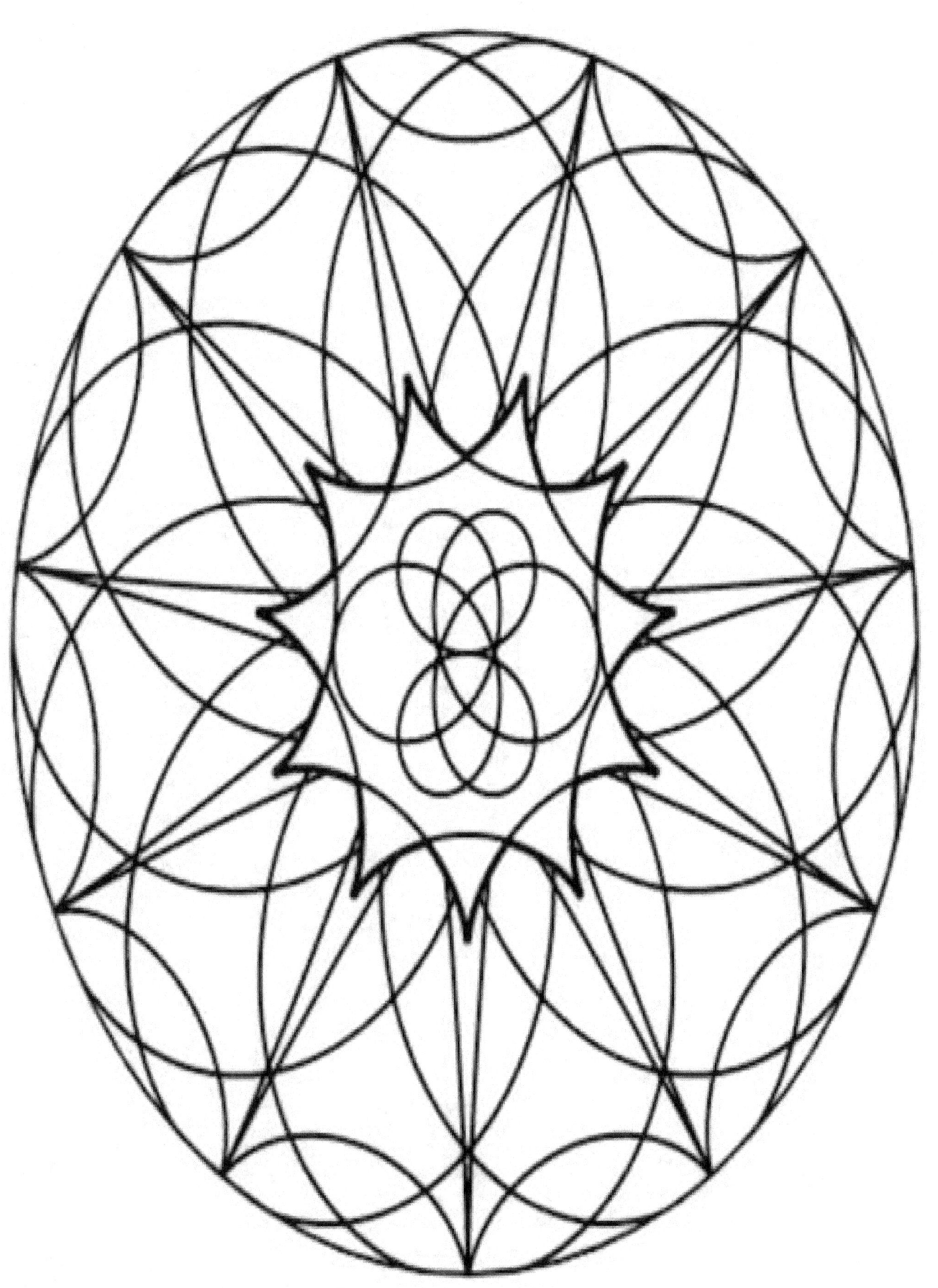

BLANK

PAGE

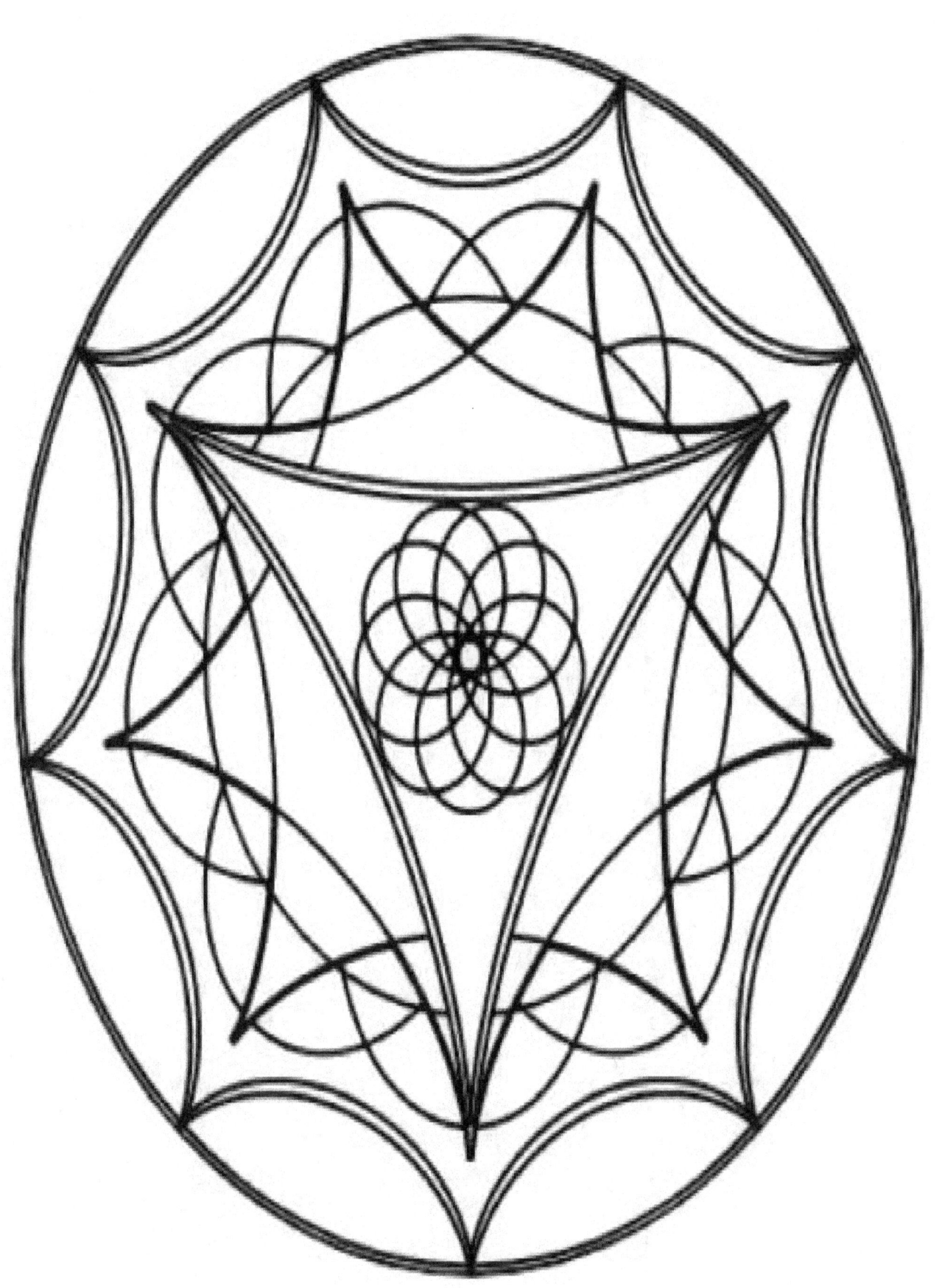

BLANK

PAGE

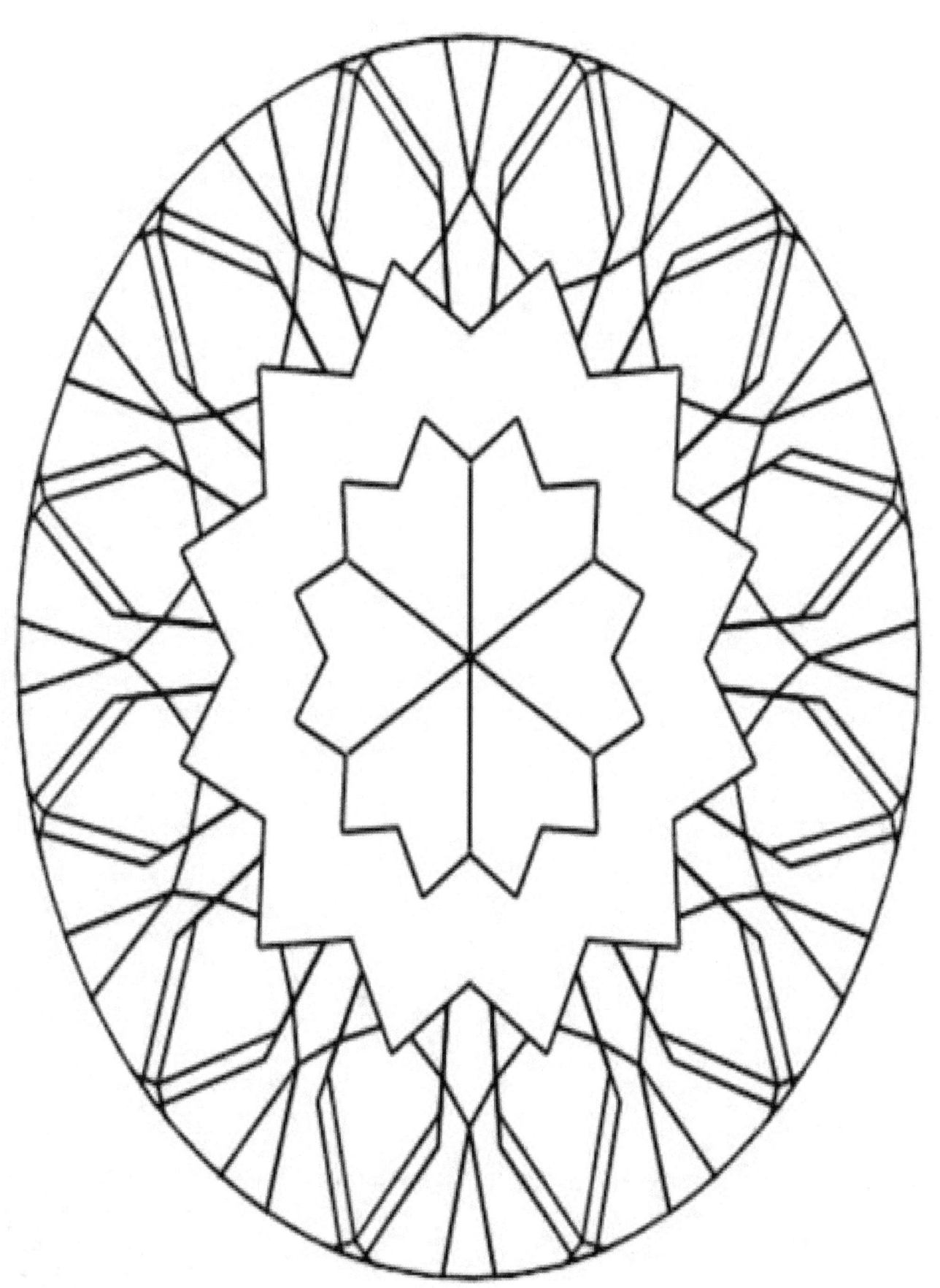

BLANK

PAGE

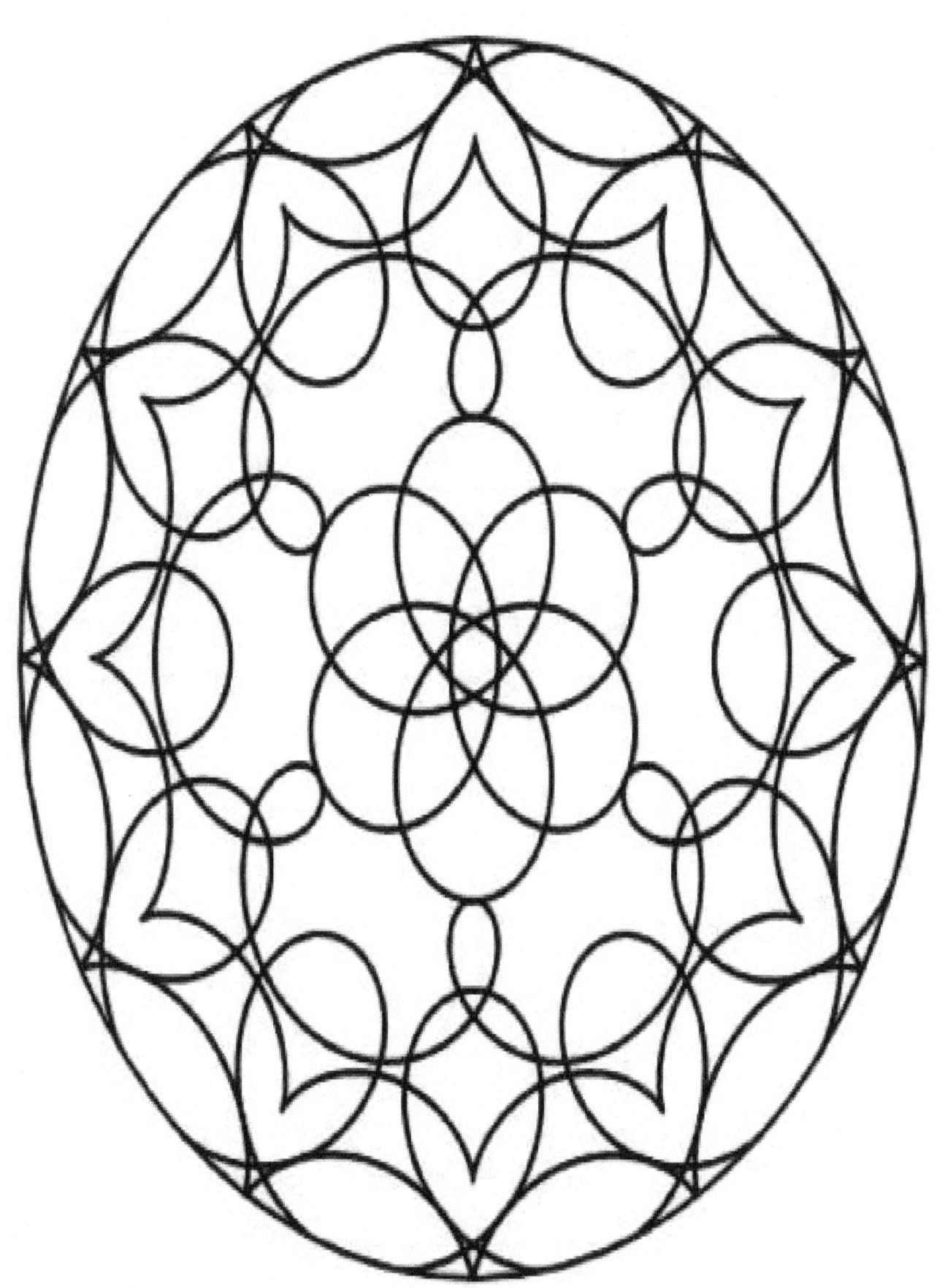

BLANK

PAGE

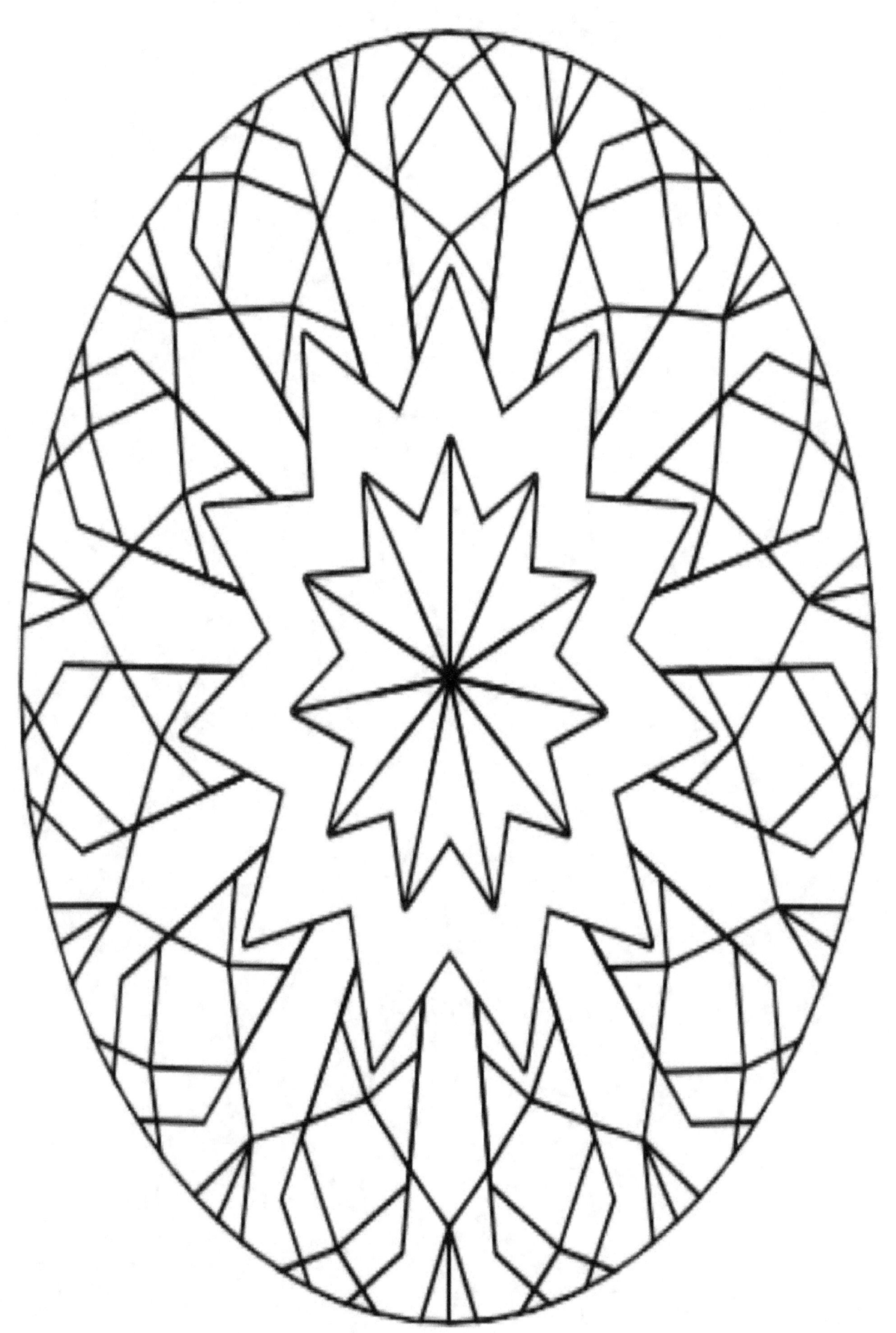

BLANK

PAGE

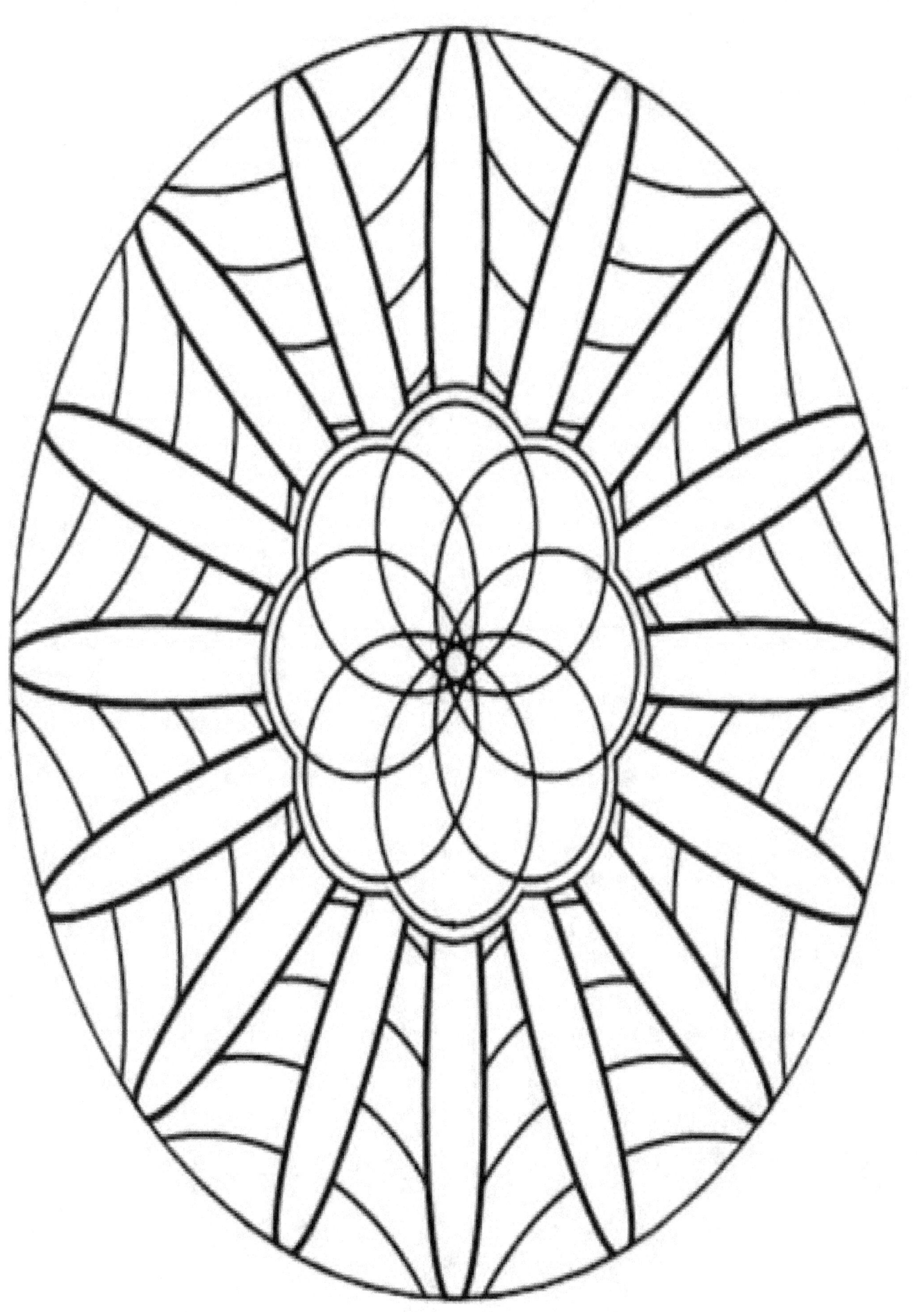

BLANK

PAGE

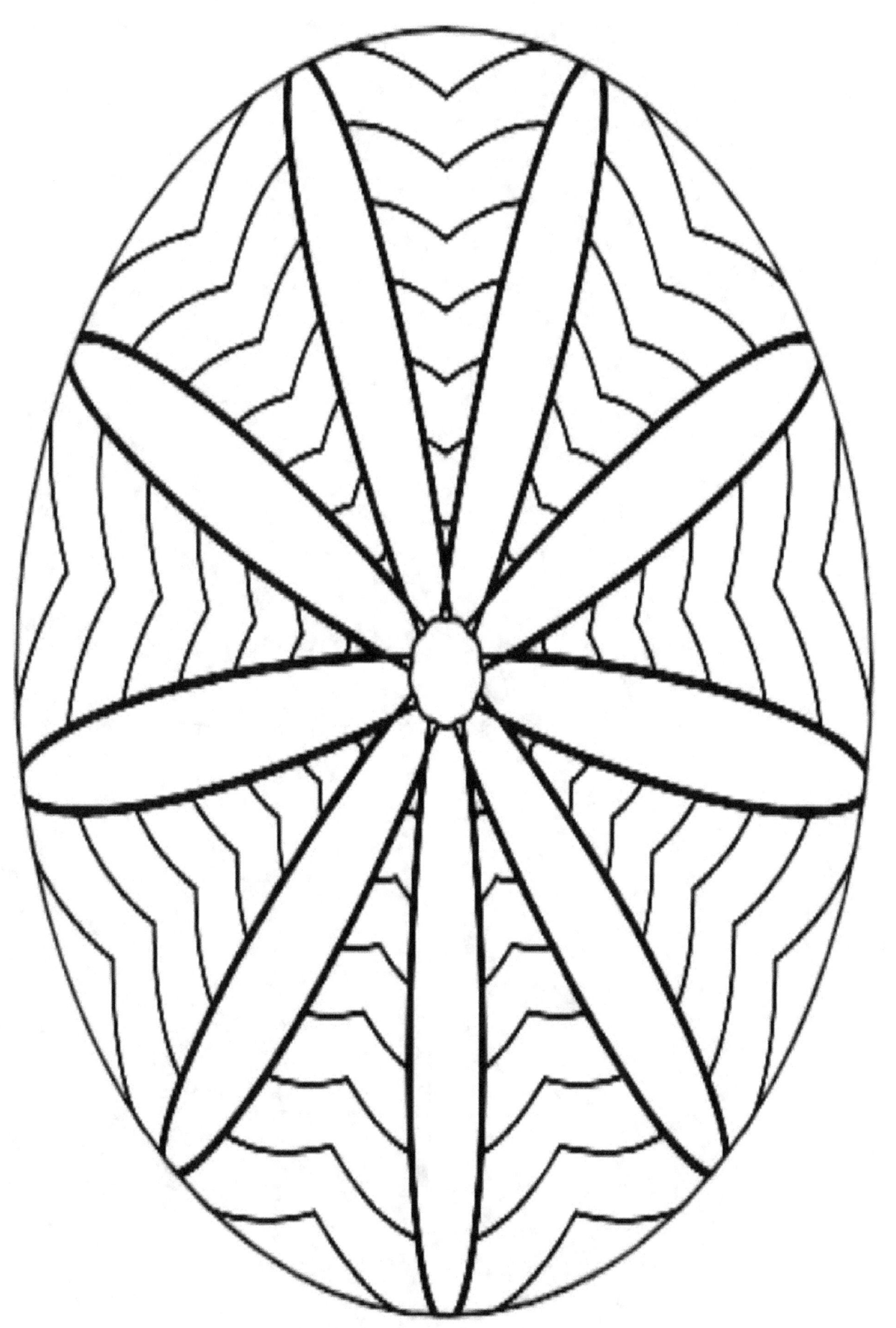

BLANK

PAGE

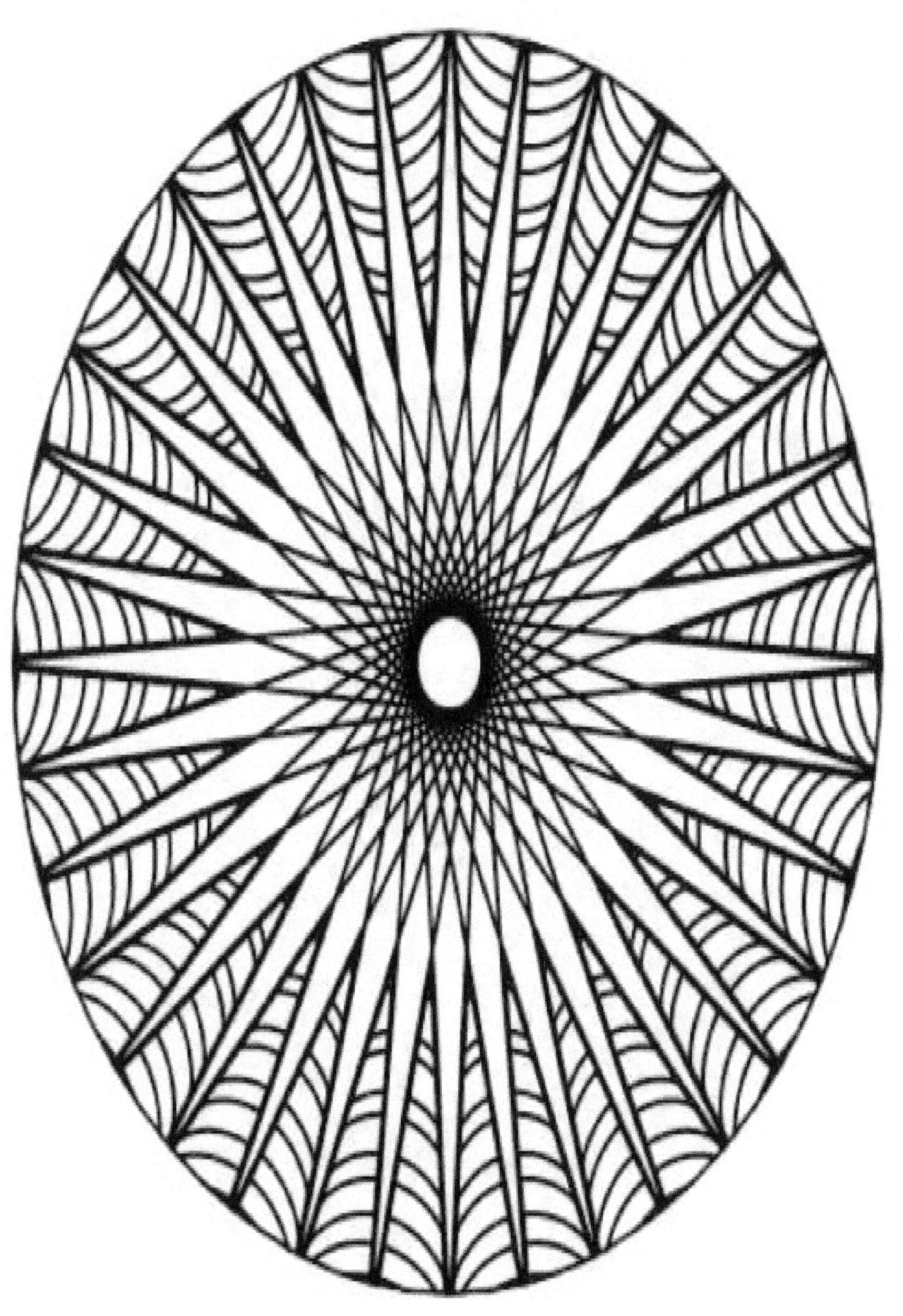

BLANK

PAGE

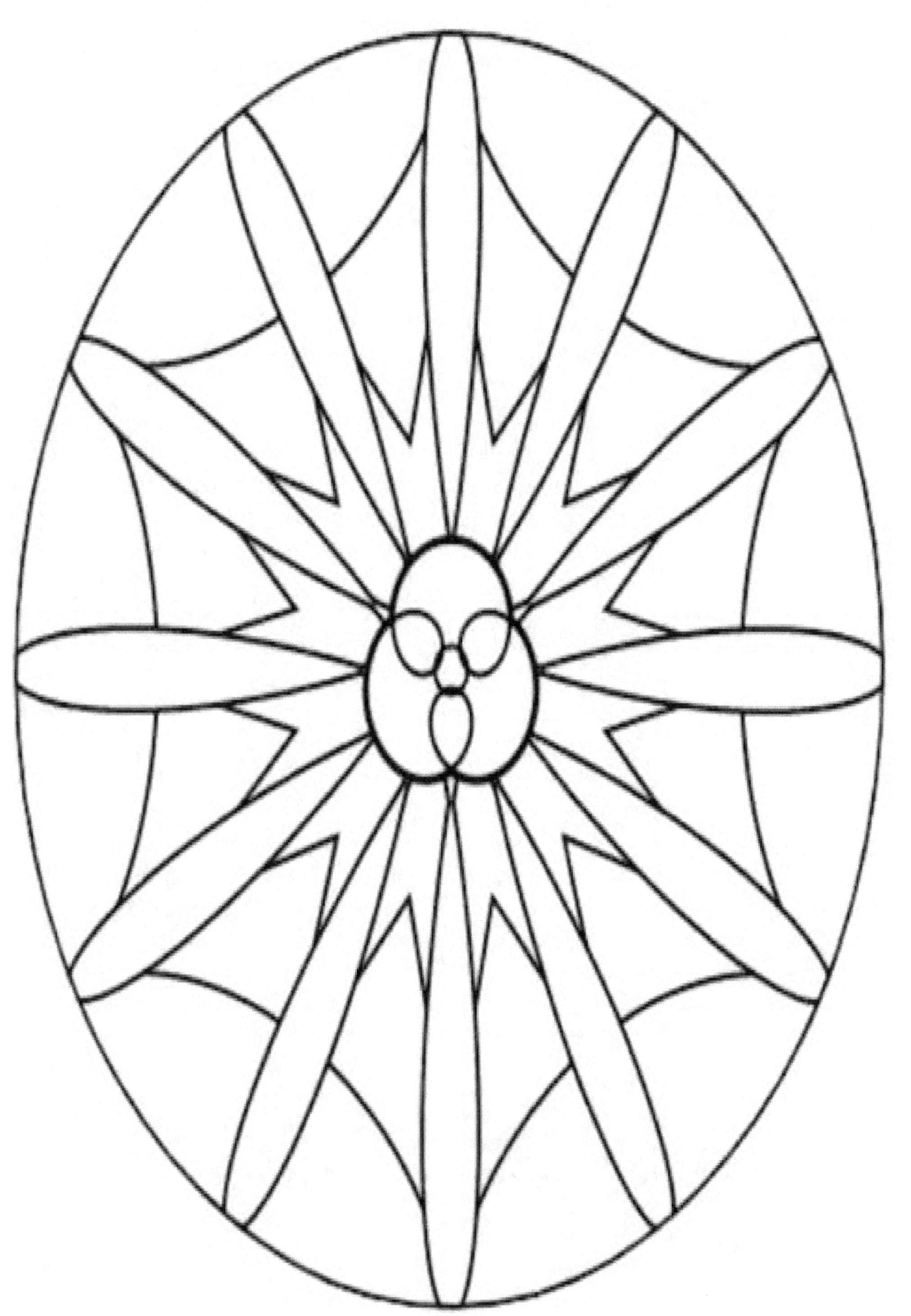

BLANK

PAGE

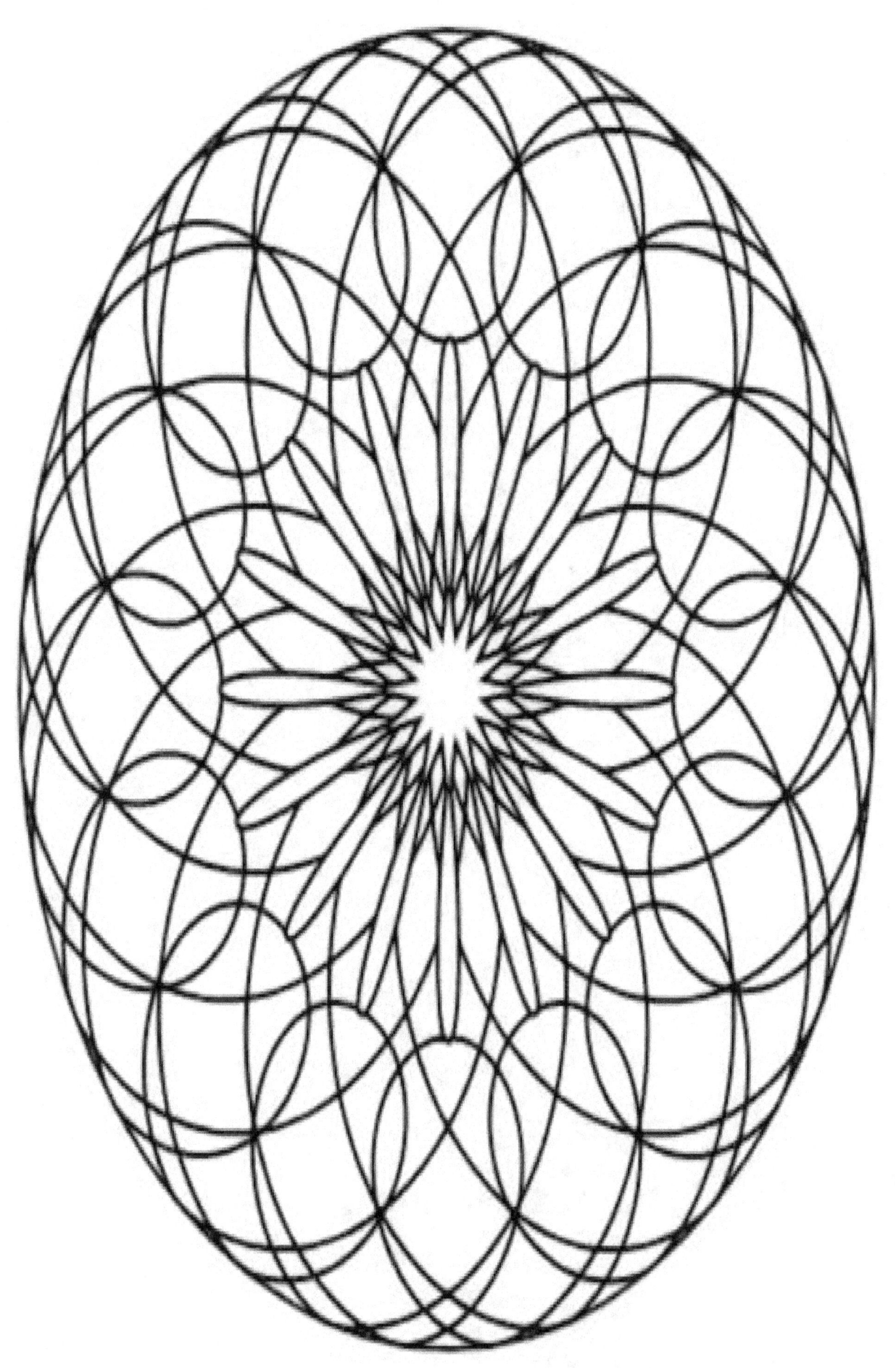

BLANK

PAGE

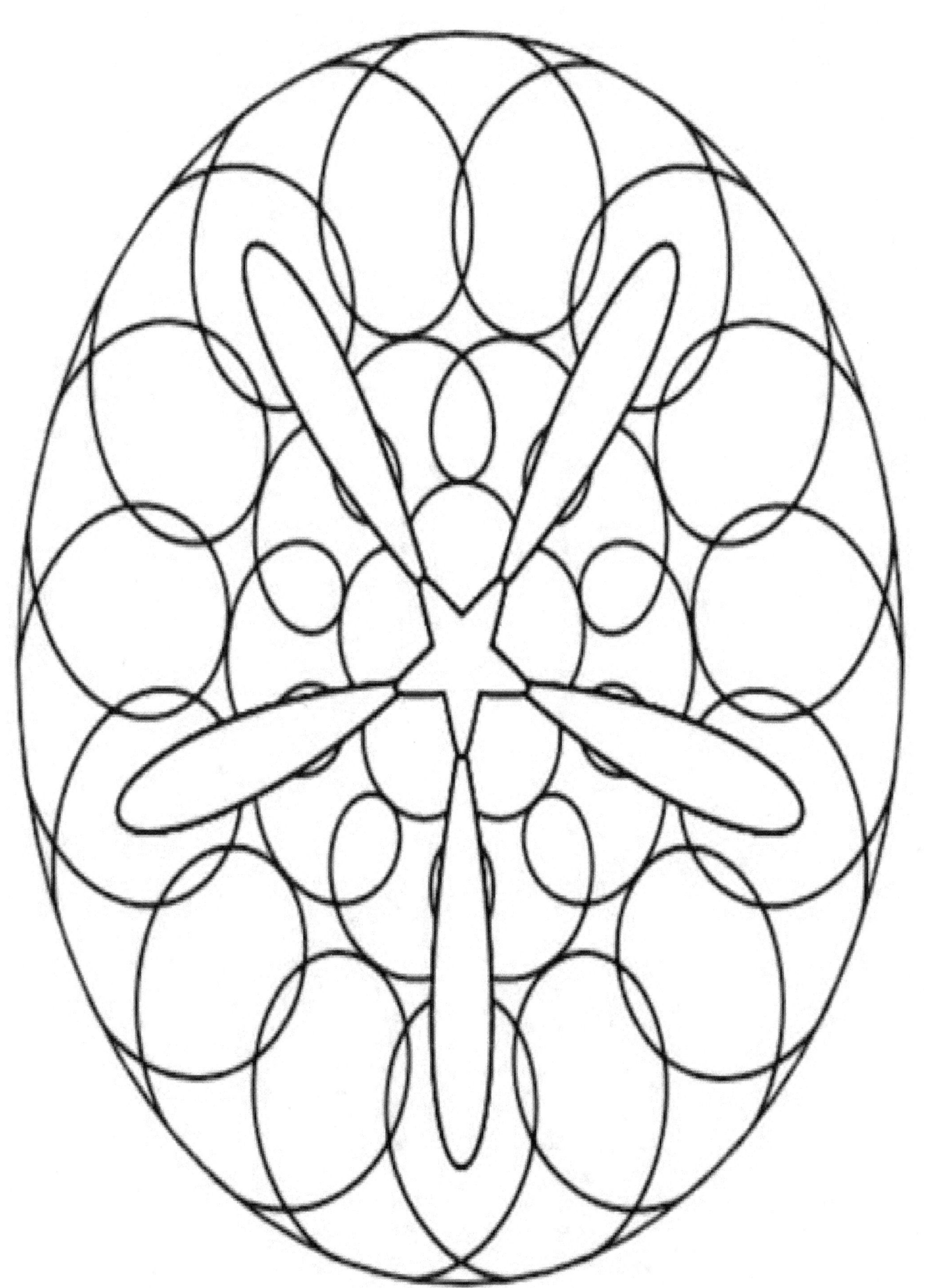

BLANK

PAGE

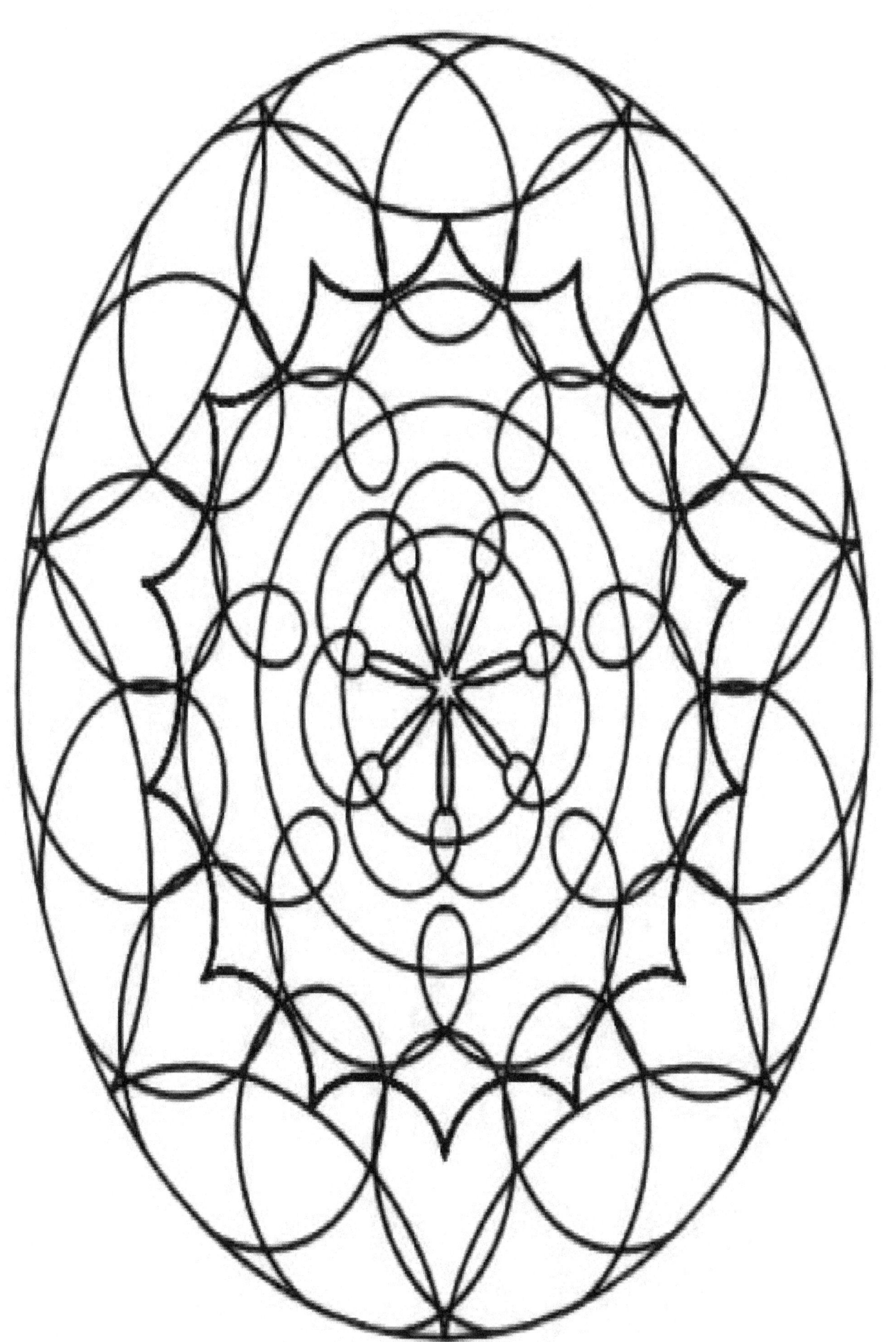

BLANK

PAGE

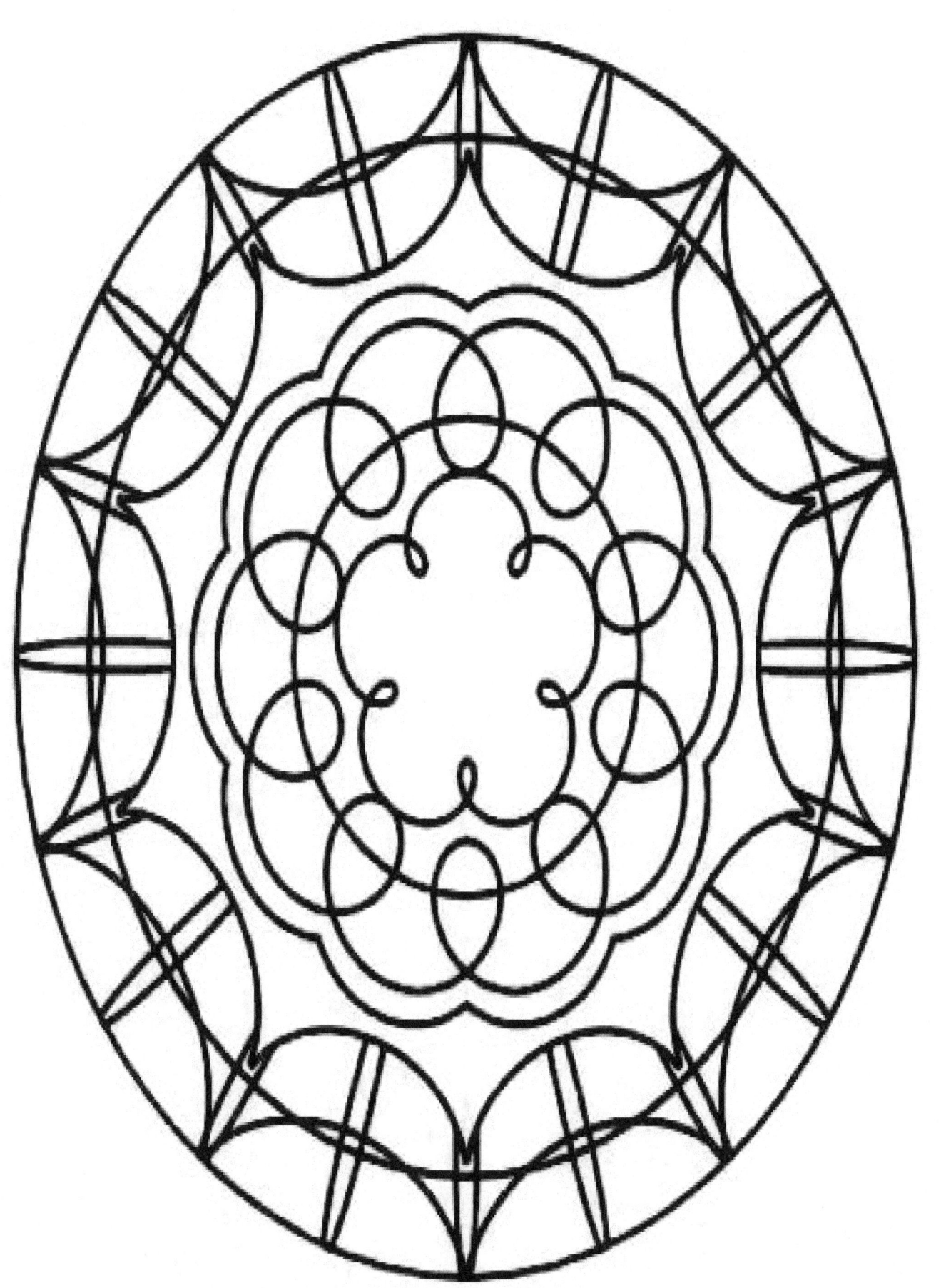

BLANK

PAGE

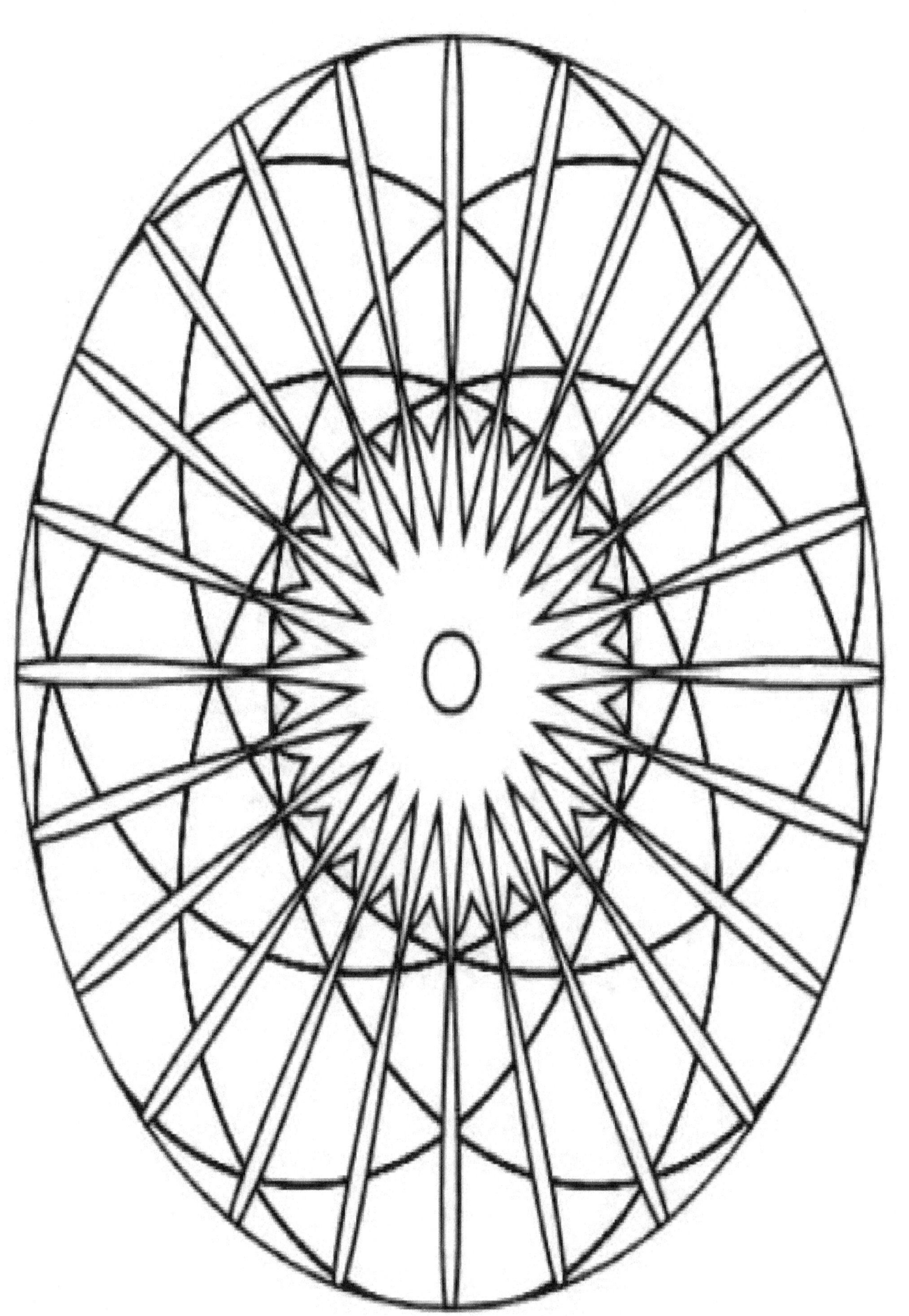

BLANK

PAGE

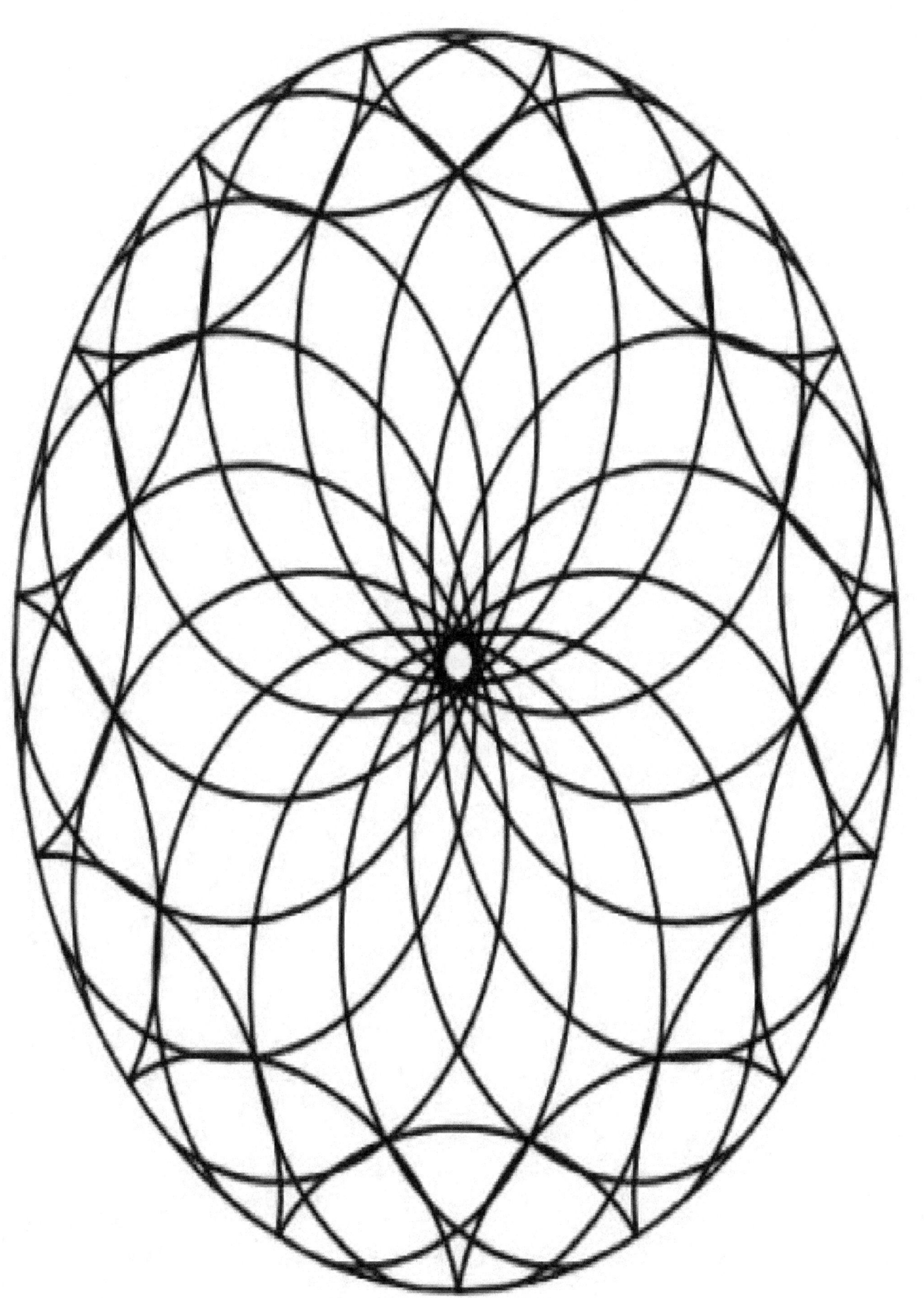

BLANK

PAGE

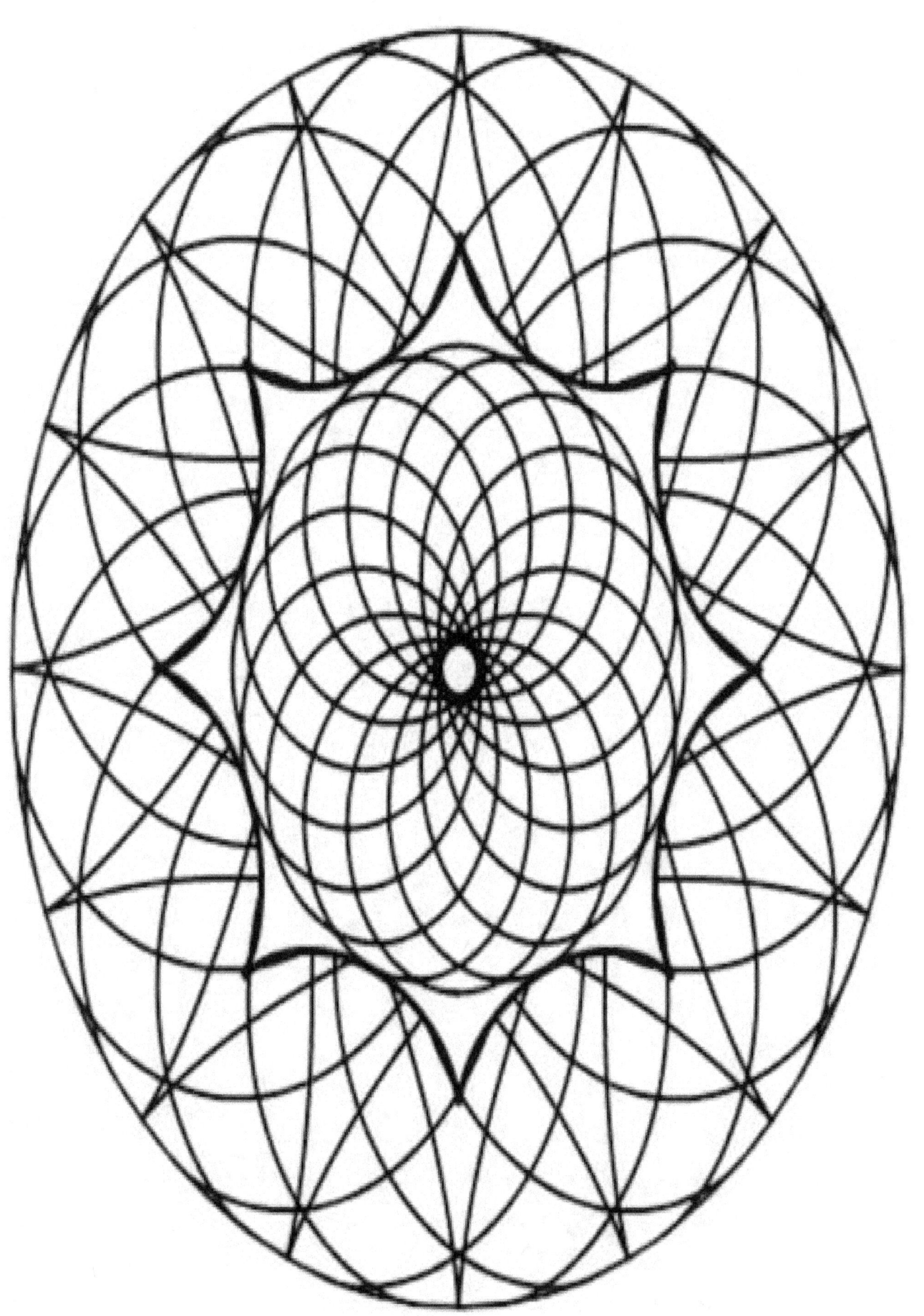

BLANK

PAGE

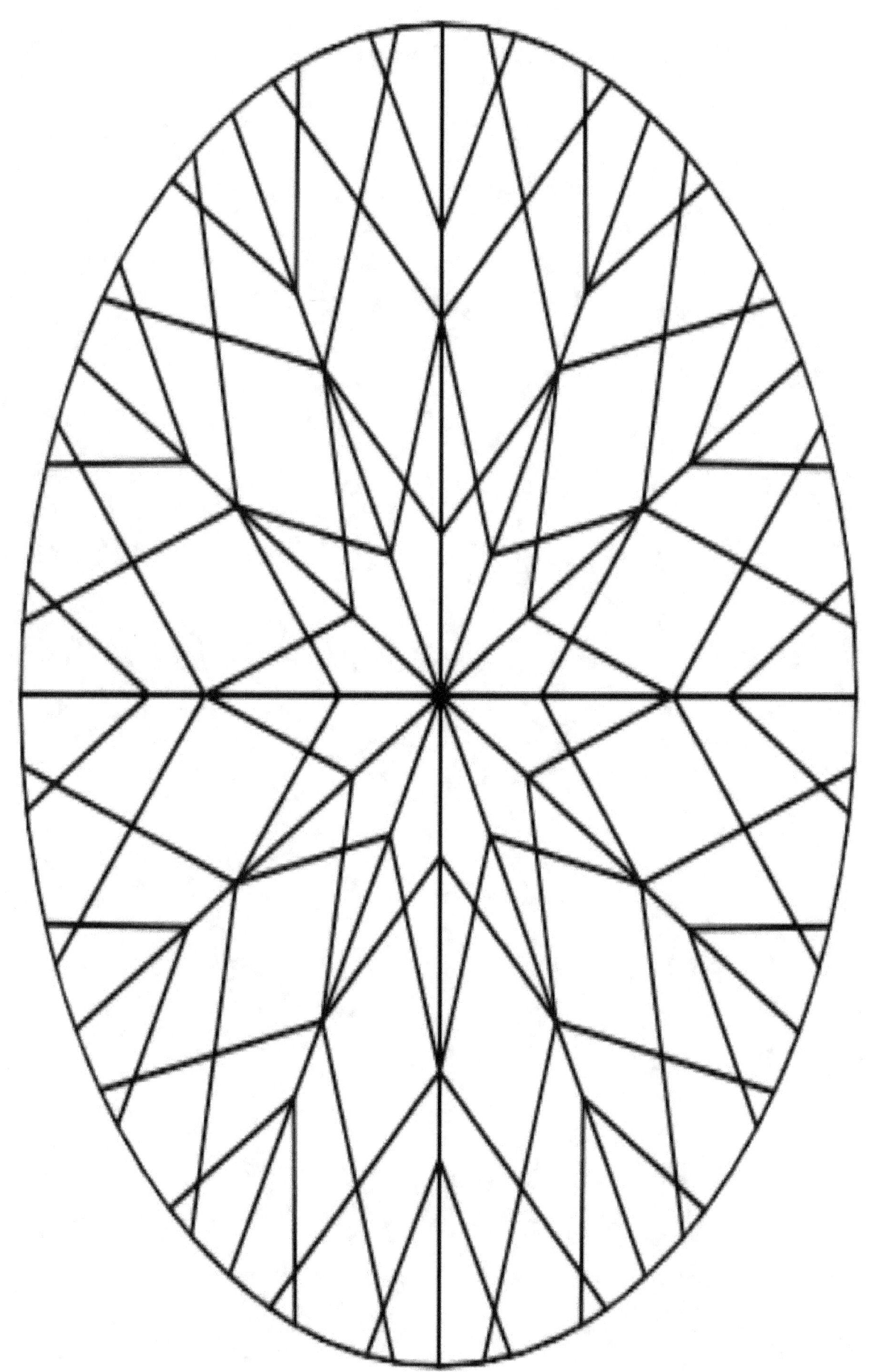

BLANK
PAGE

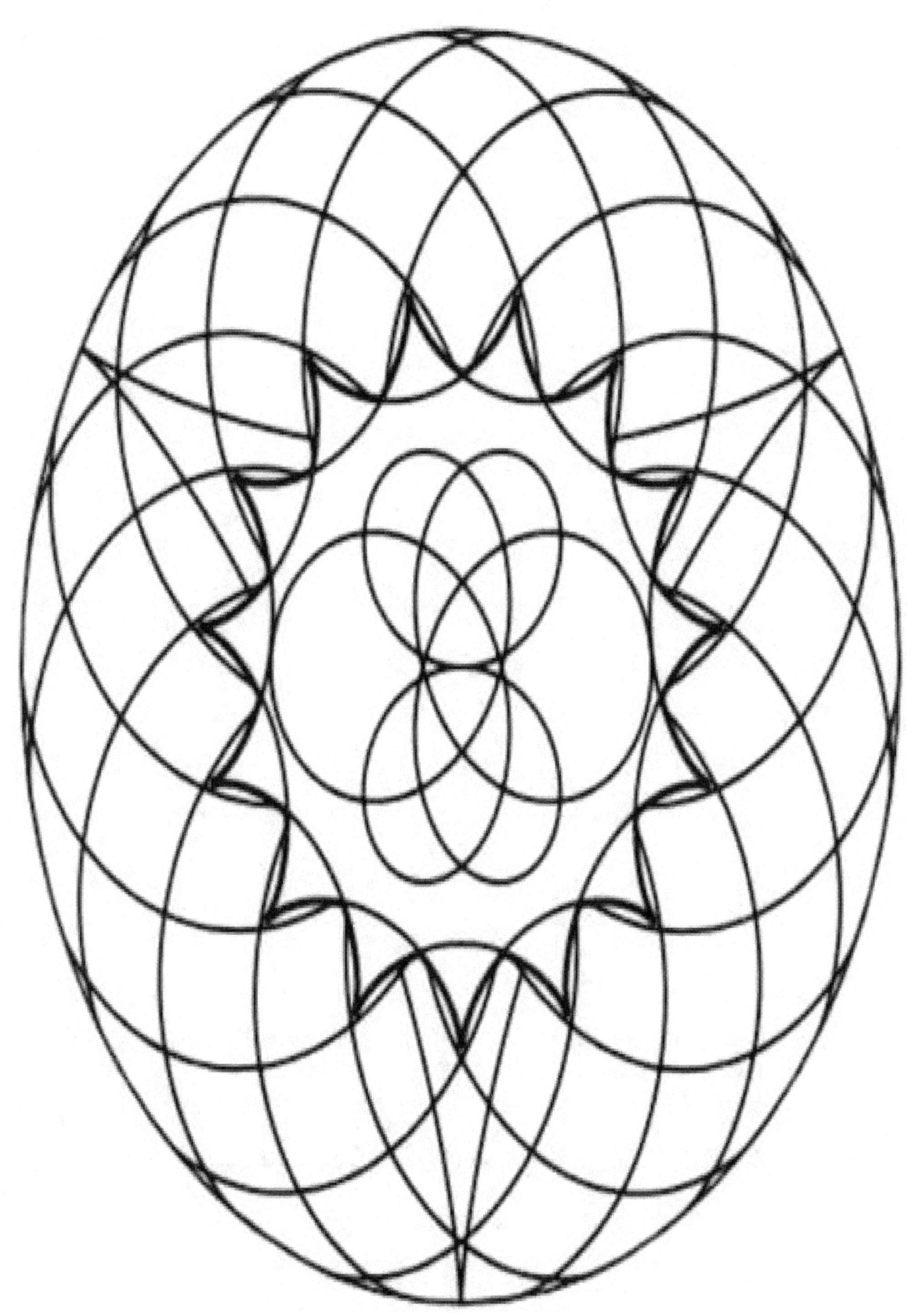

BLANK

PAGE

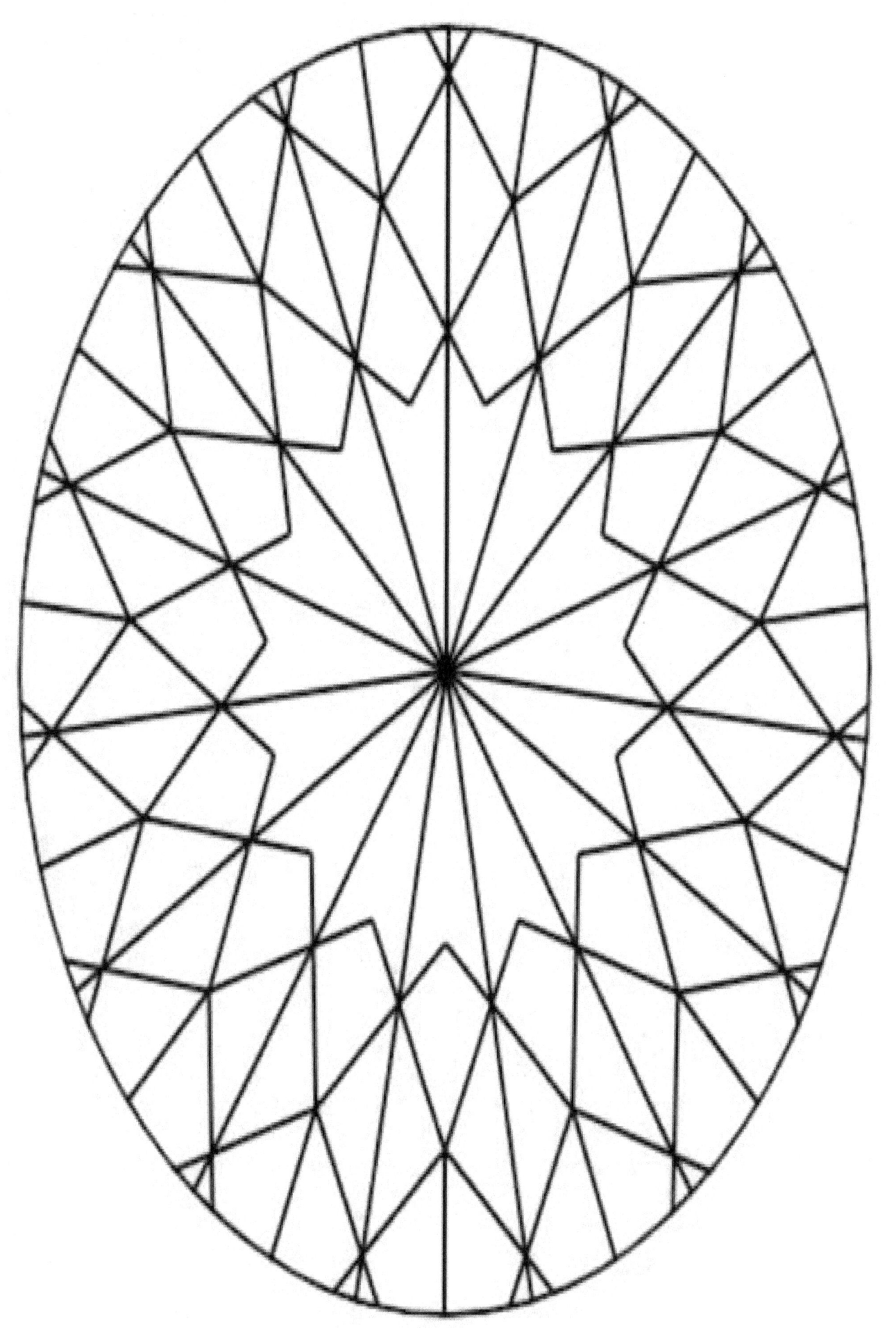

BLANK

PAGE

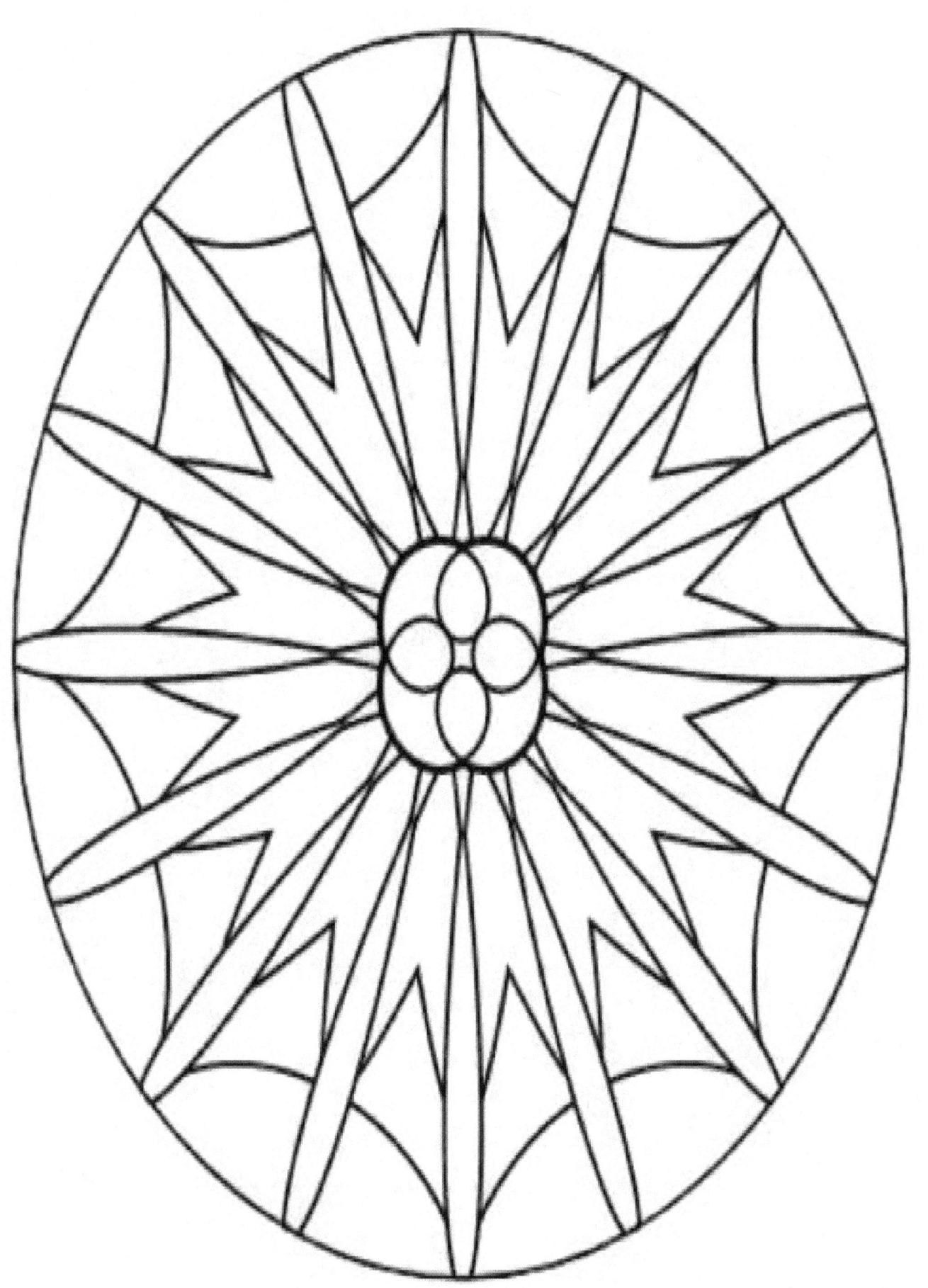

BLANK

PAGE

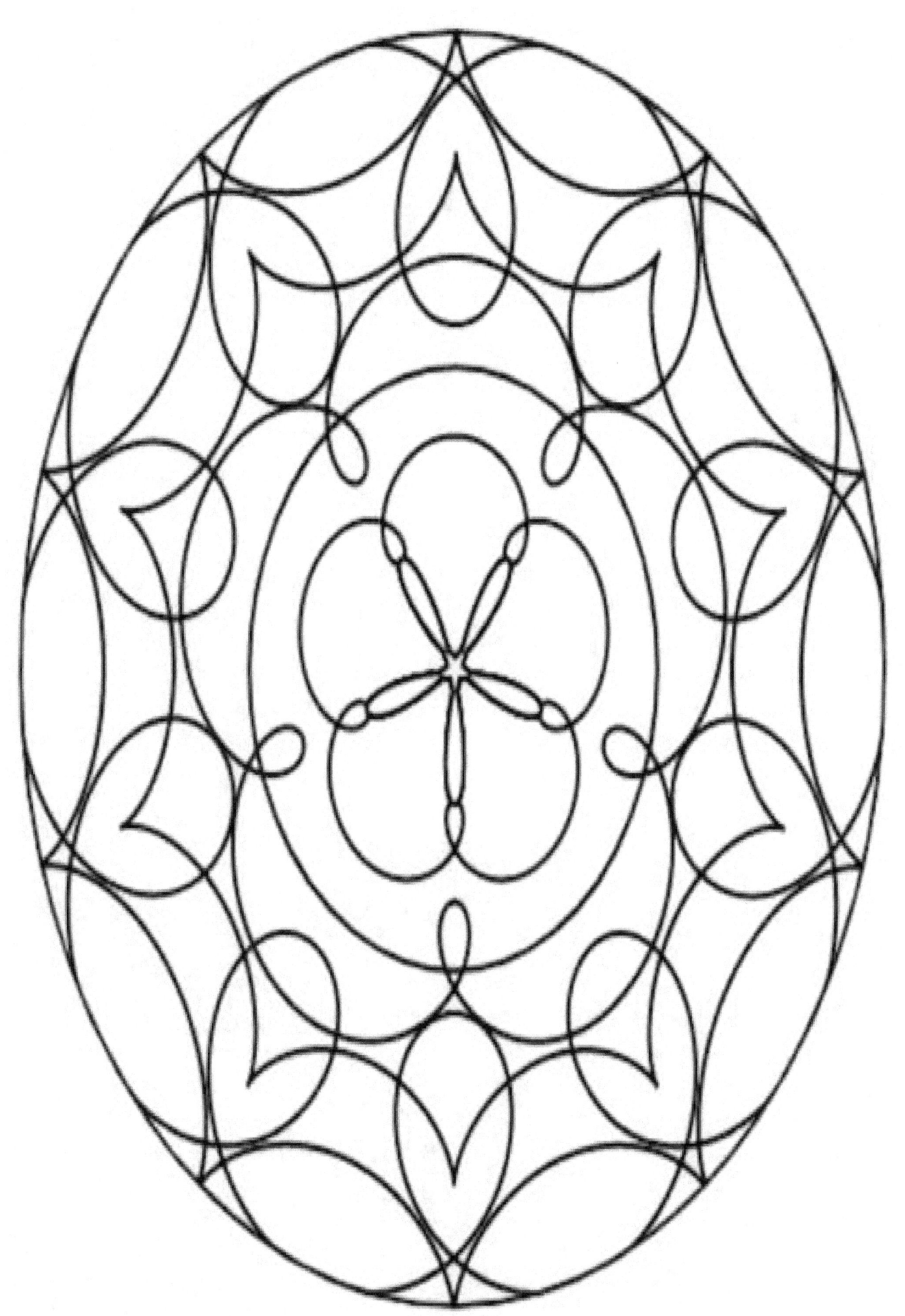

BLANK

PAGE

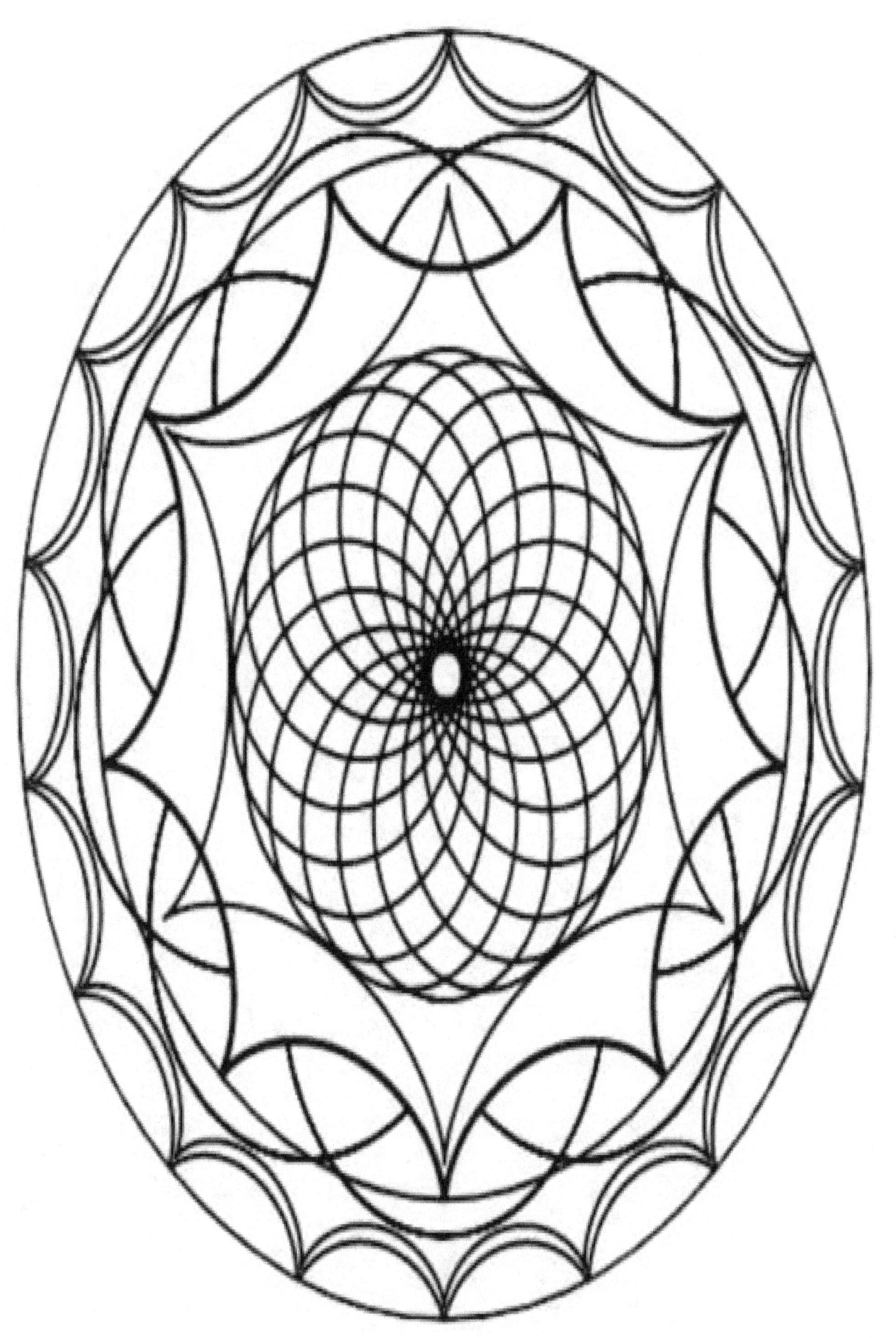

BLANK

PAGE

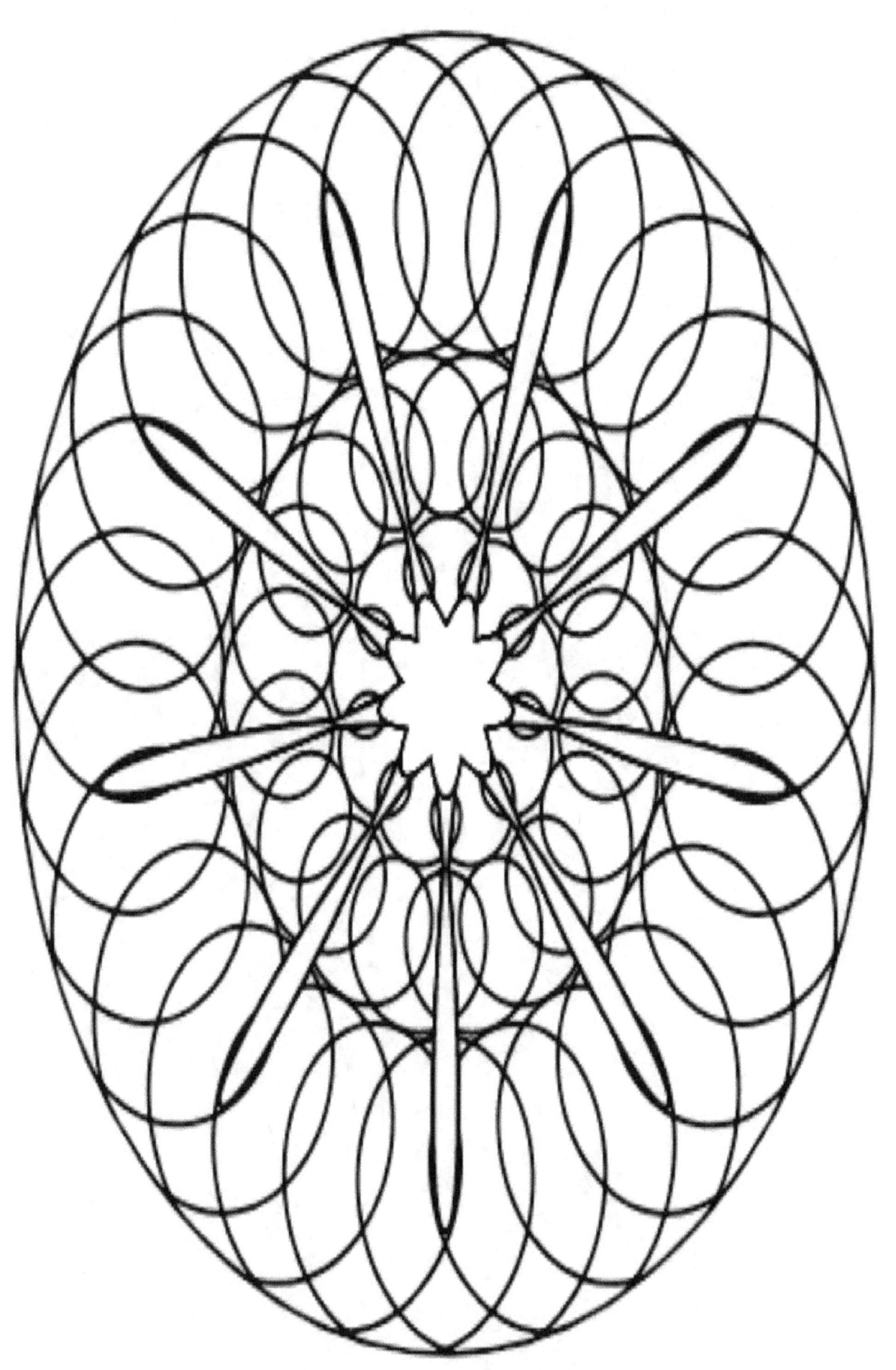

BLANK

PAGE

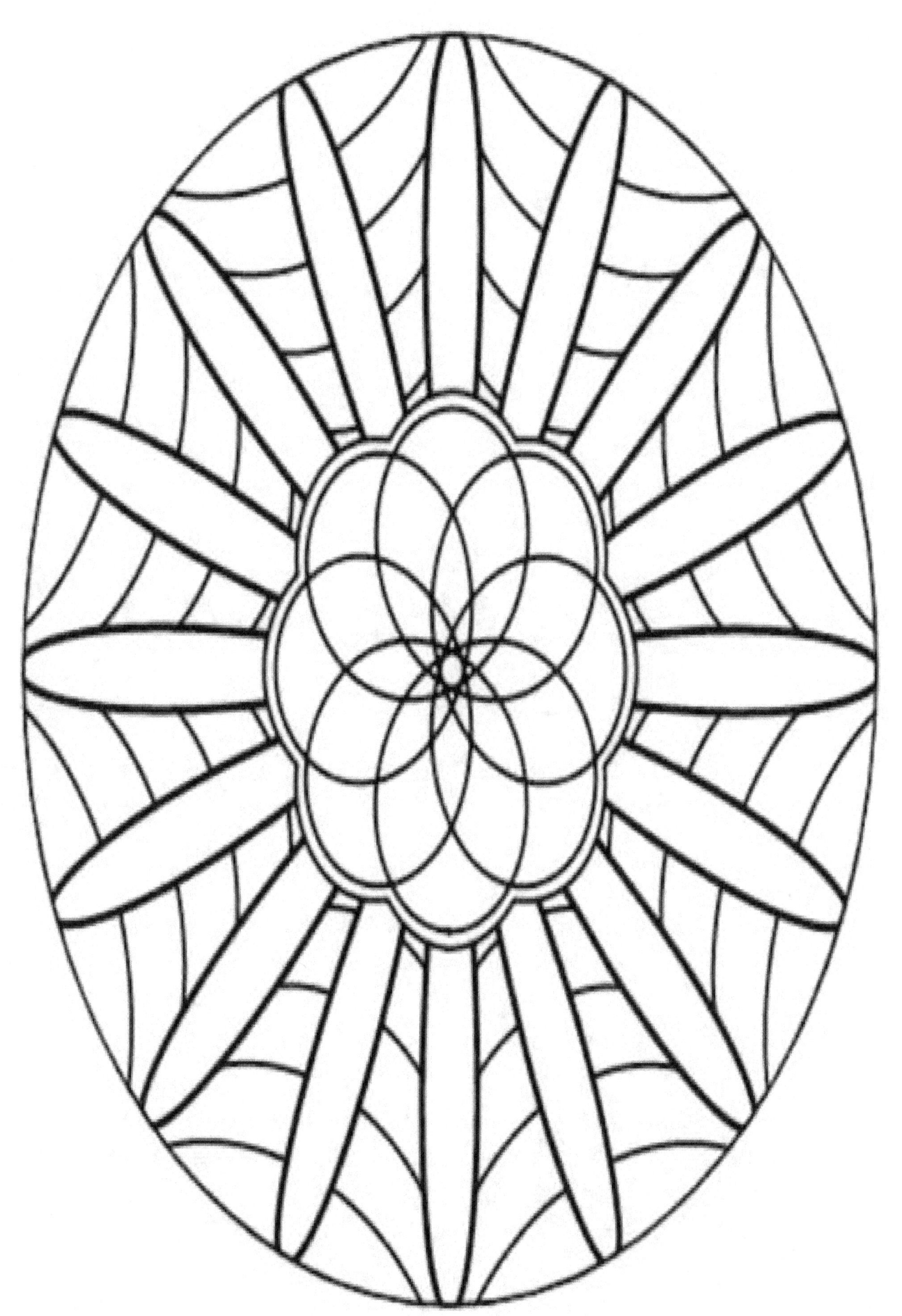

BLANK

PAGE

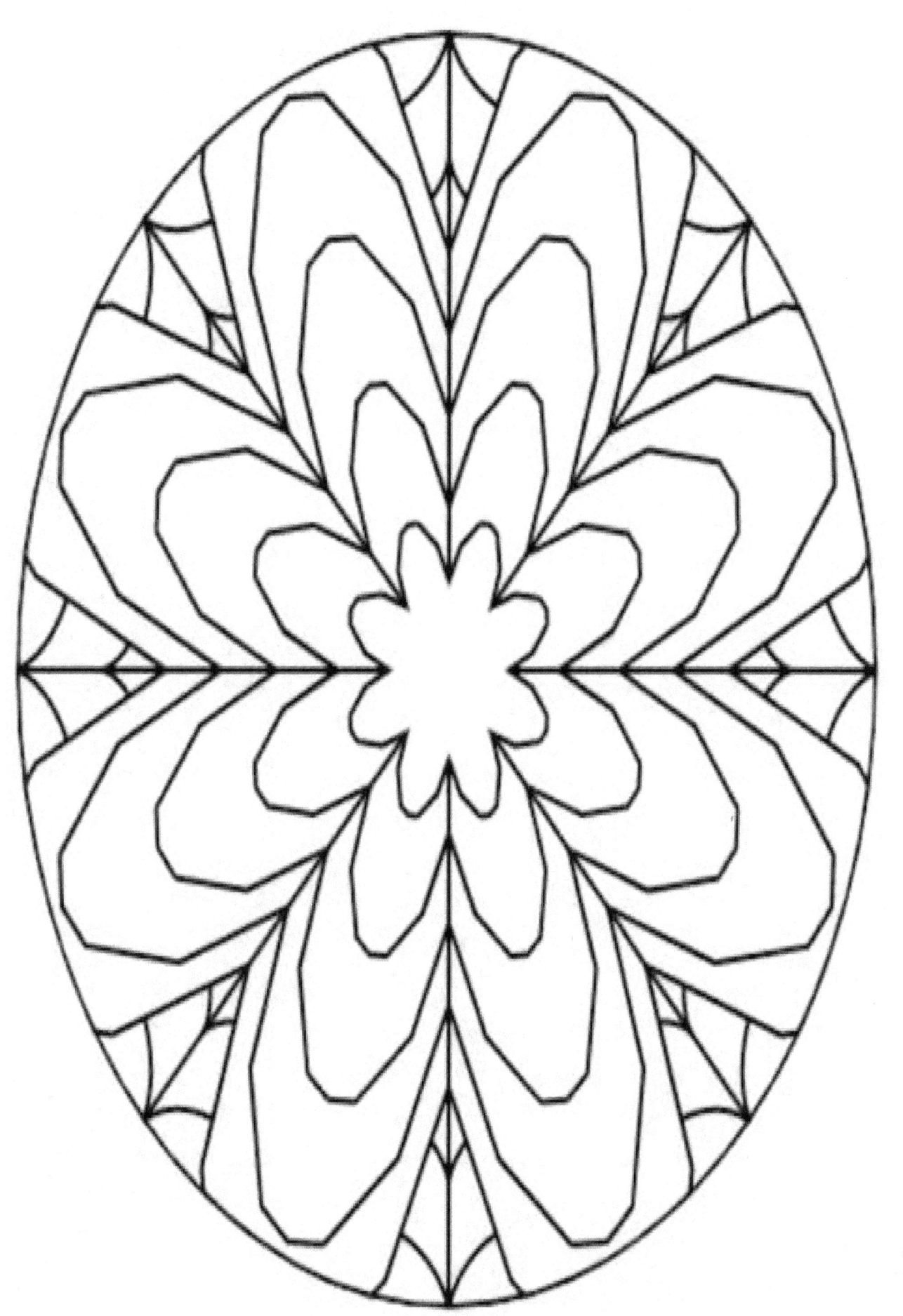

BLANK

PAGE

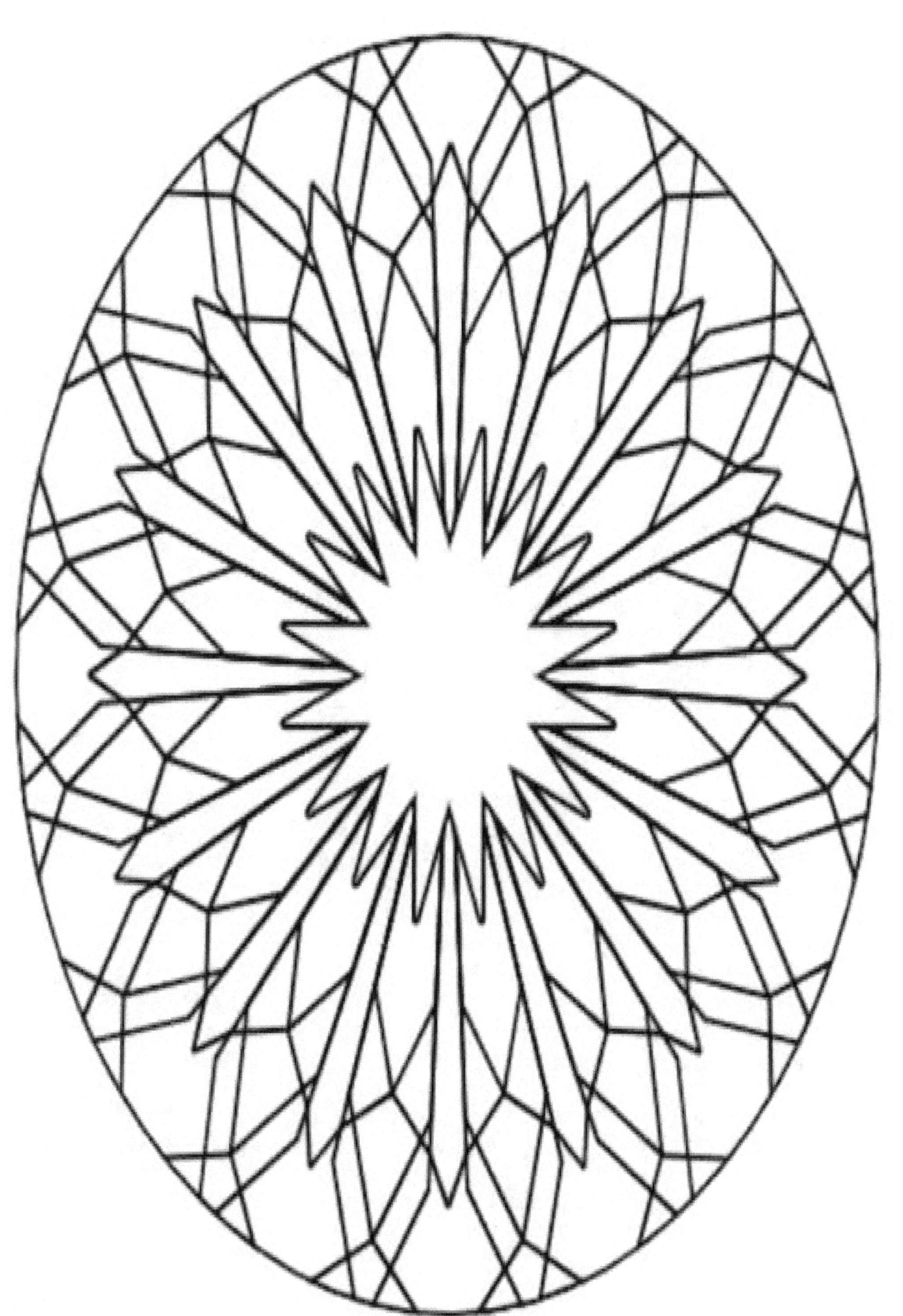

BLANK

PAGE

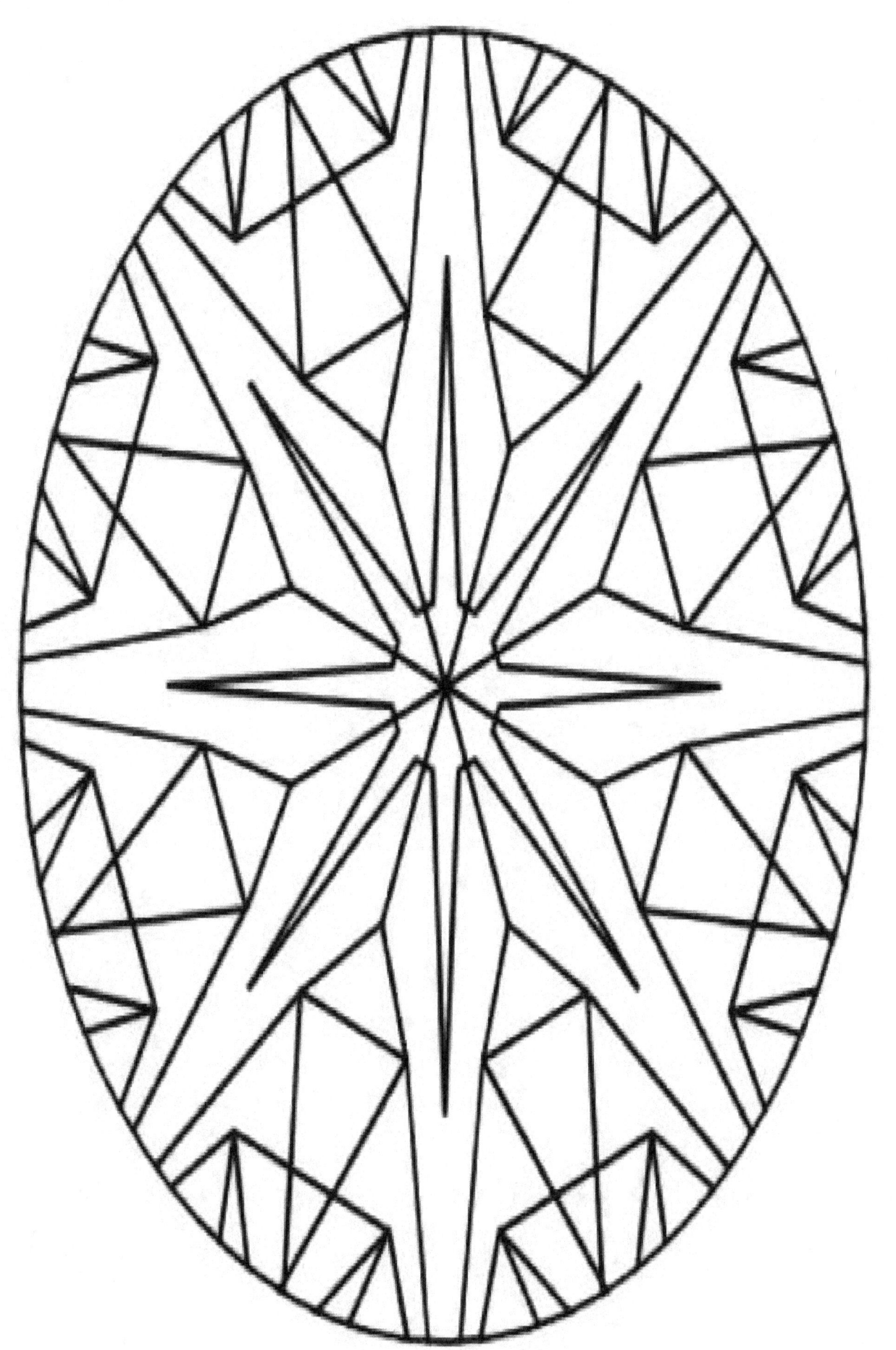

BLANK

PAGE

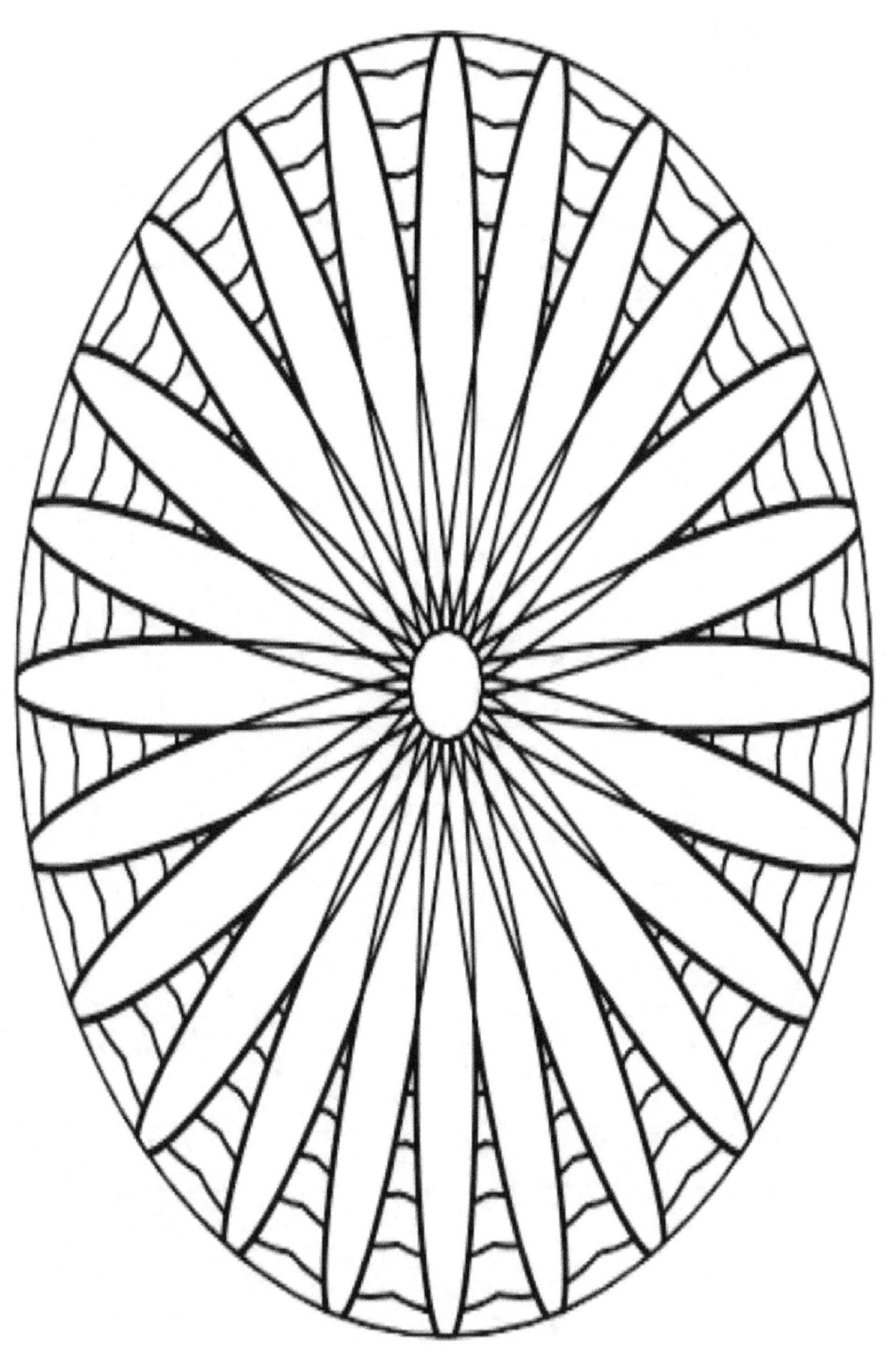

BLANK

PAGE

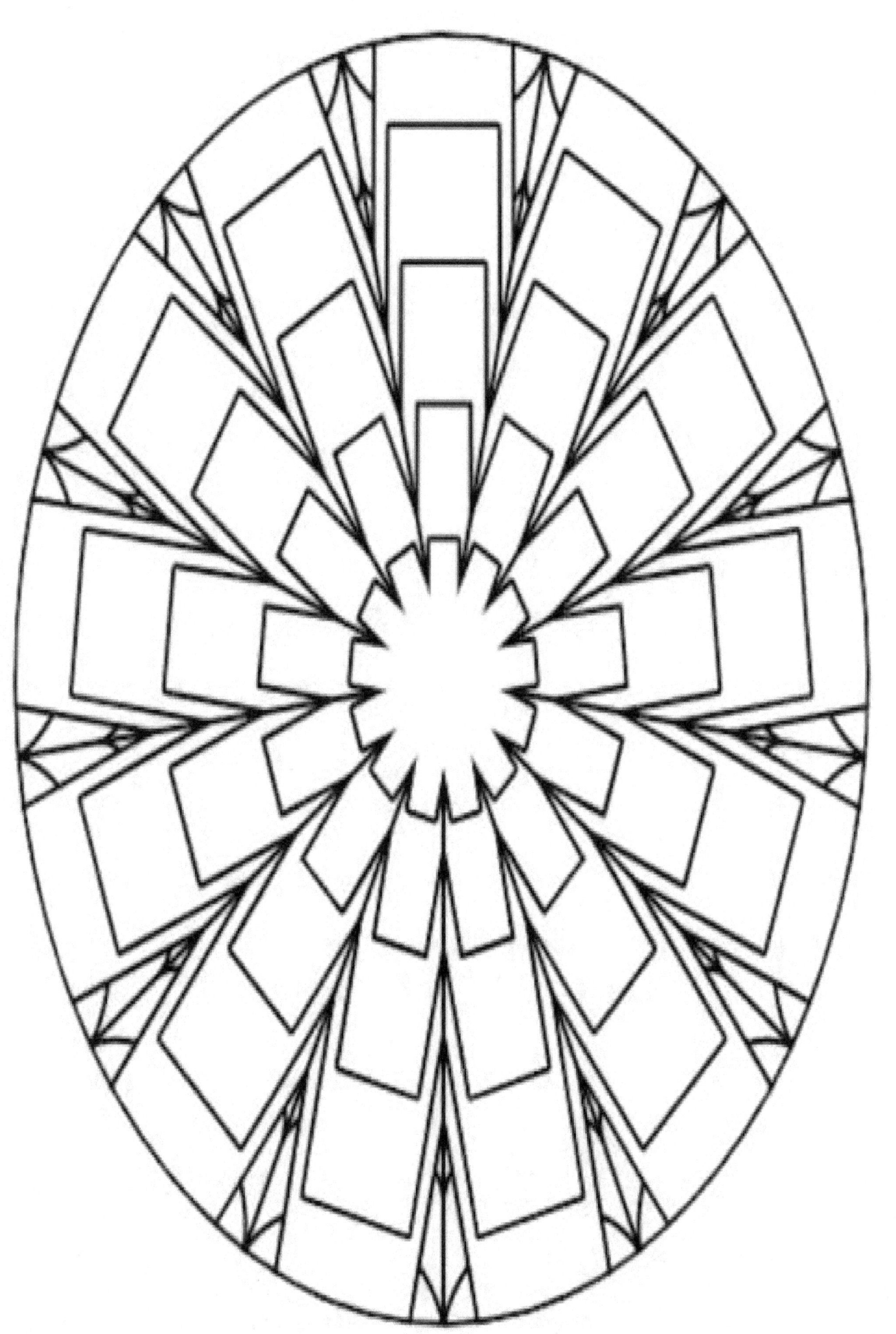

BLANK PAGE

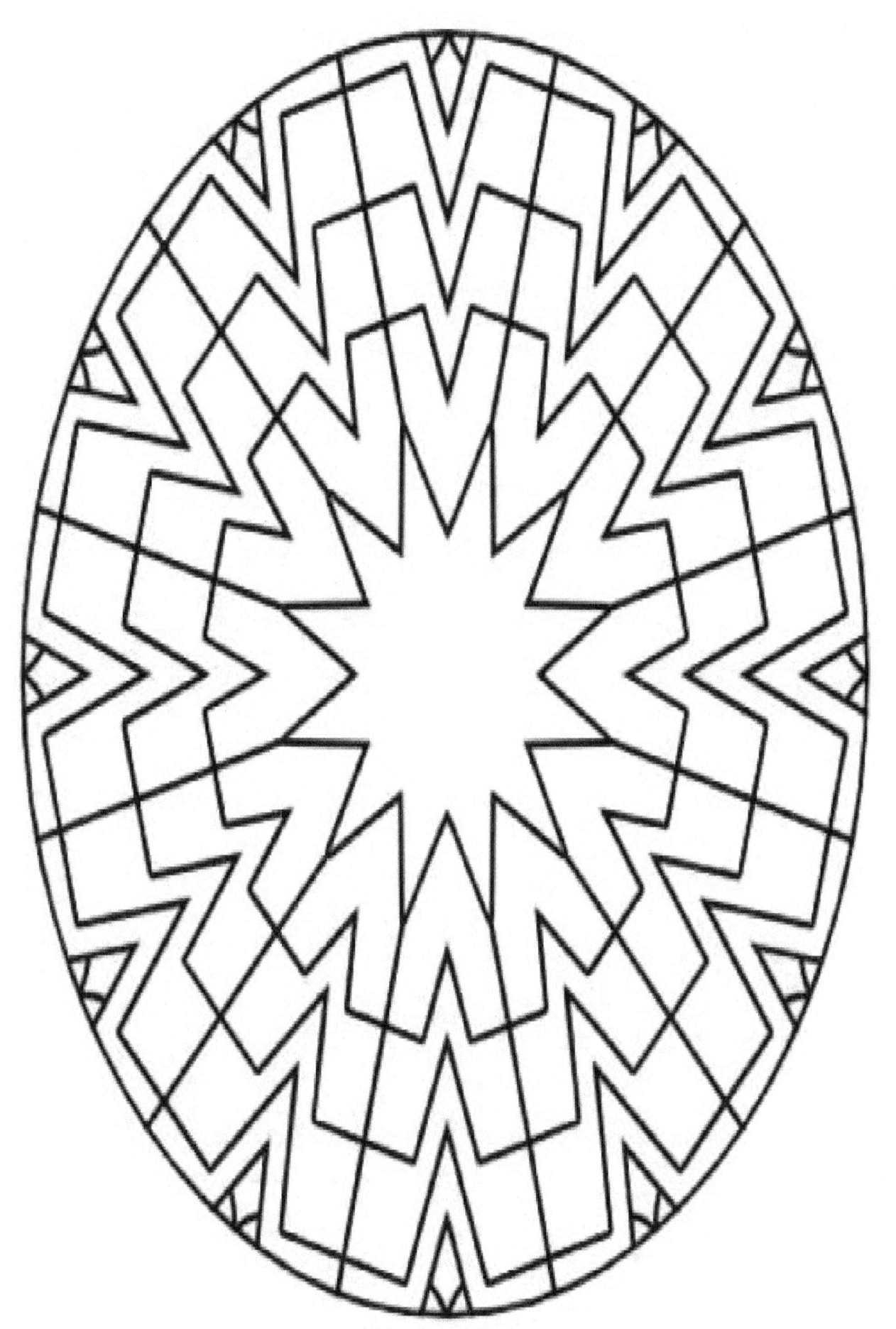

BLANK

PAGE

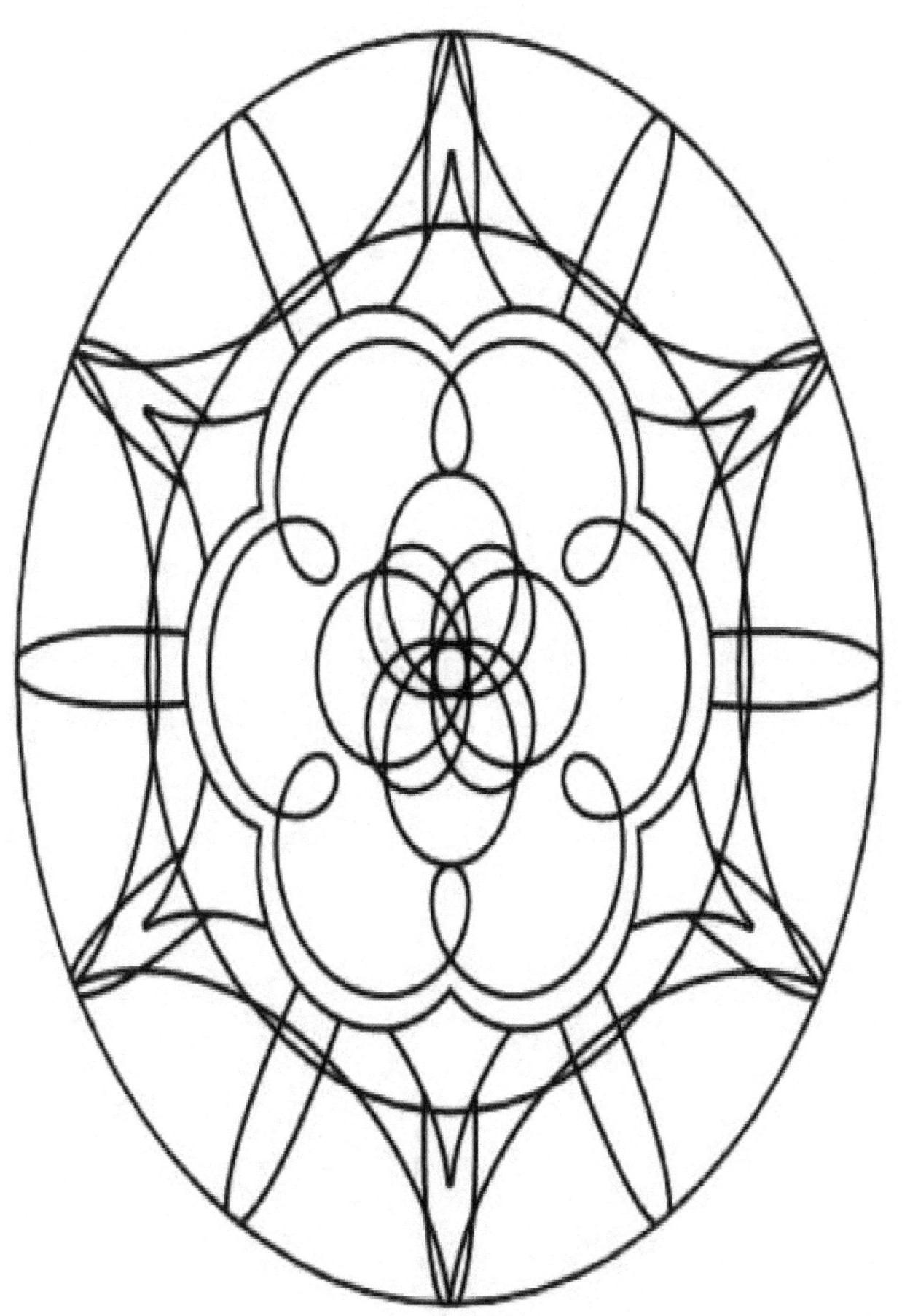

BLANK PAGE

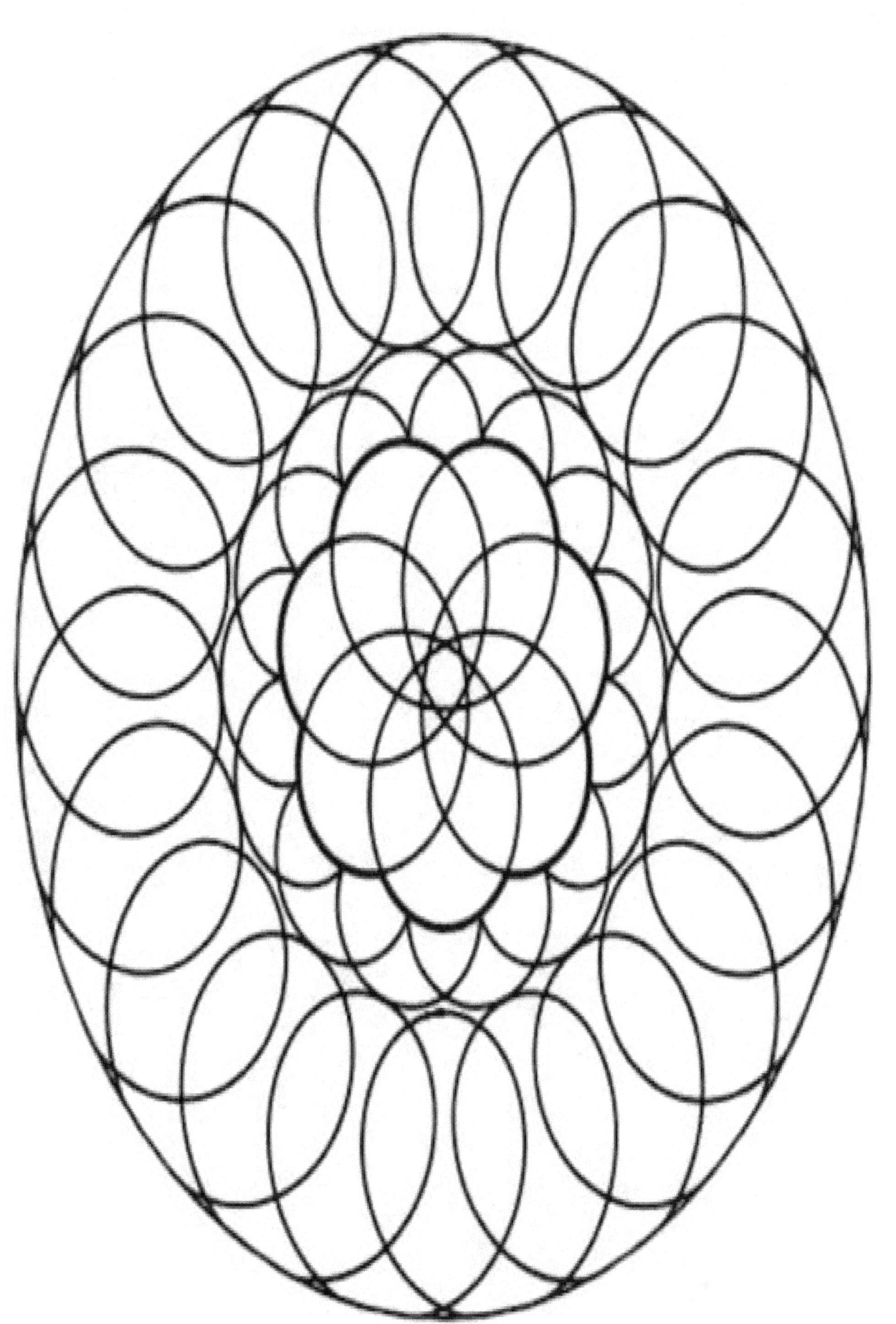

BLANK

PAGE

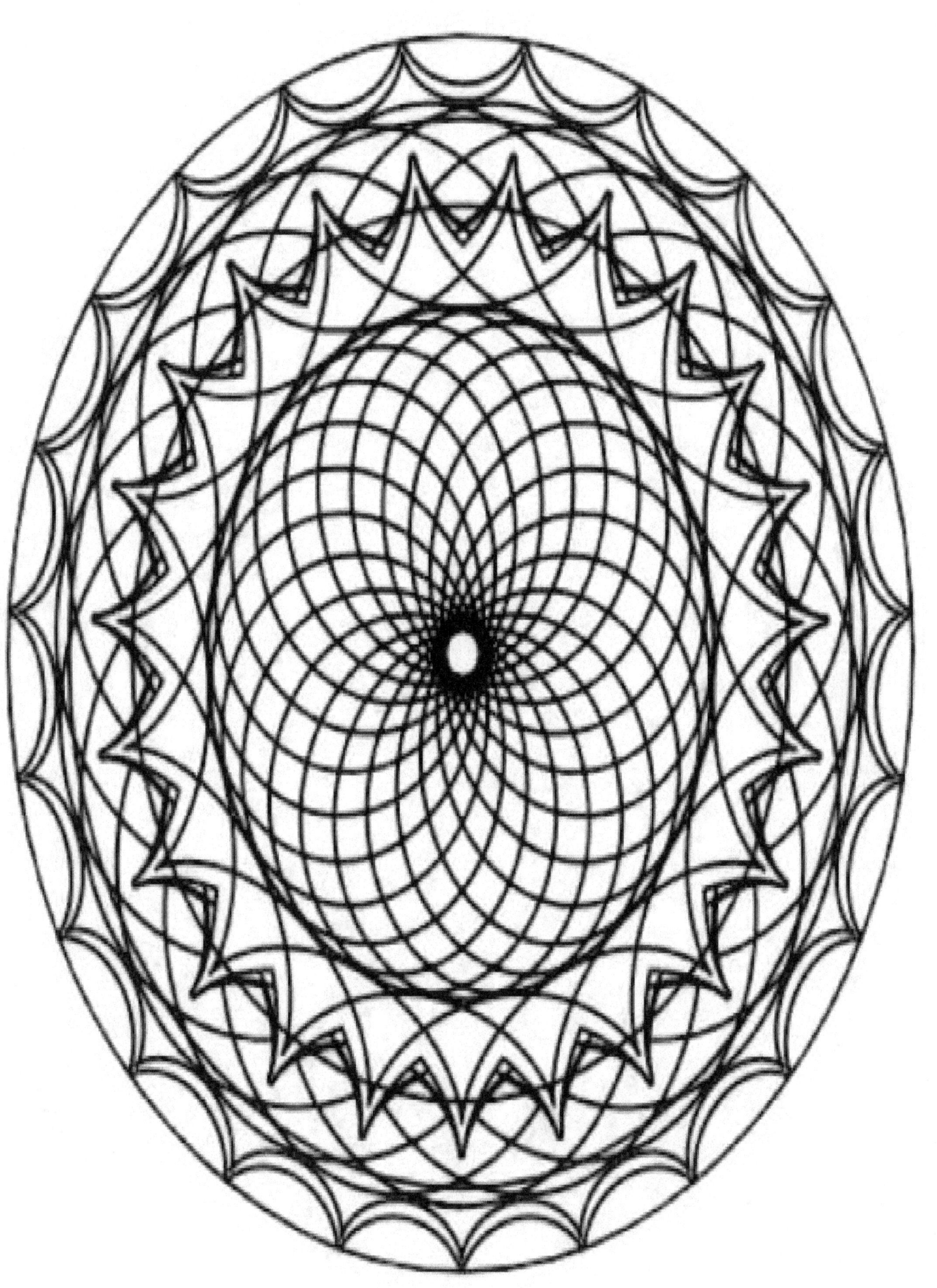

BLANK

PAGE

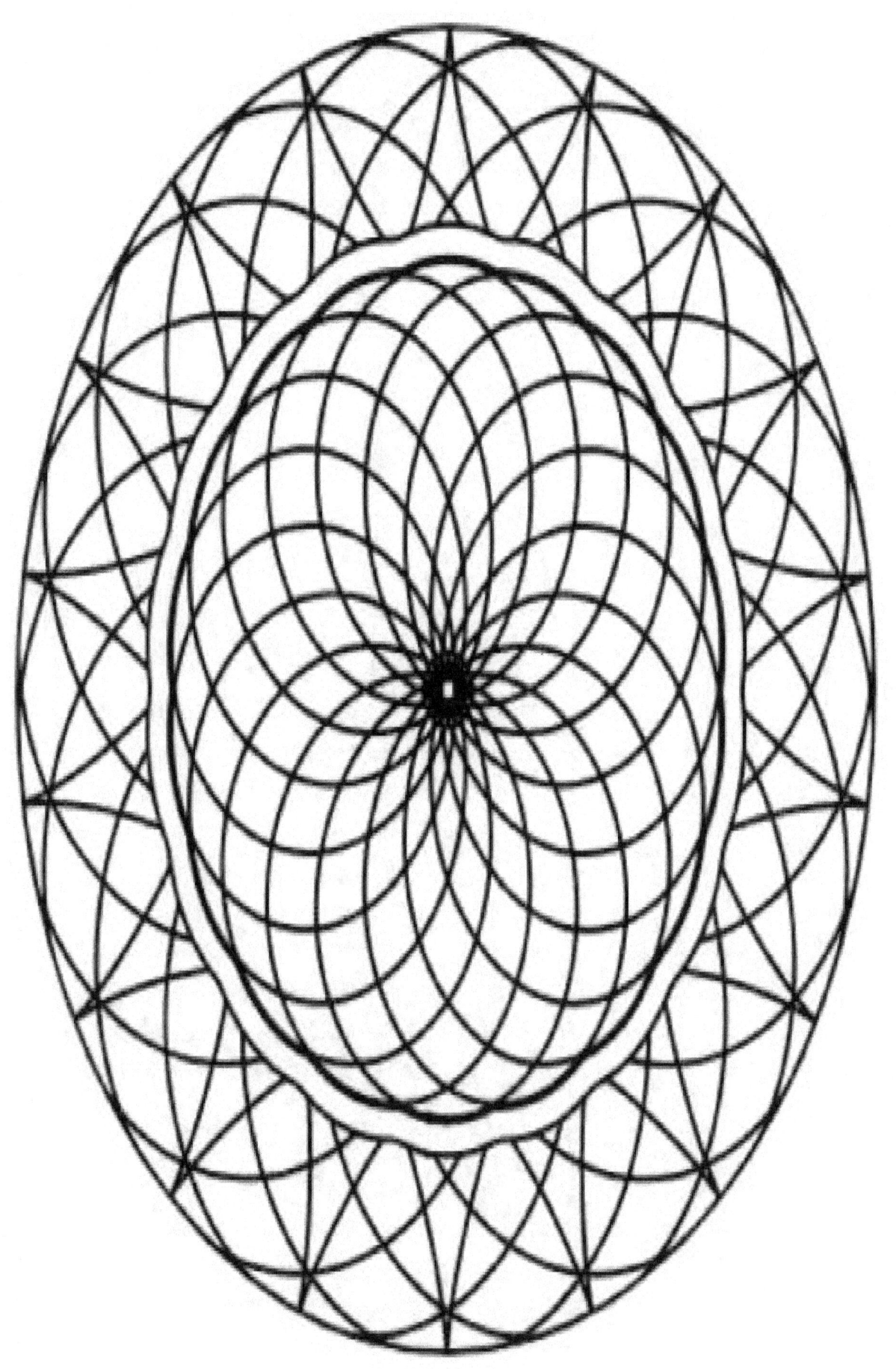

BLANK PAGE

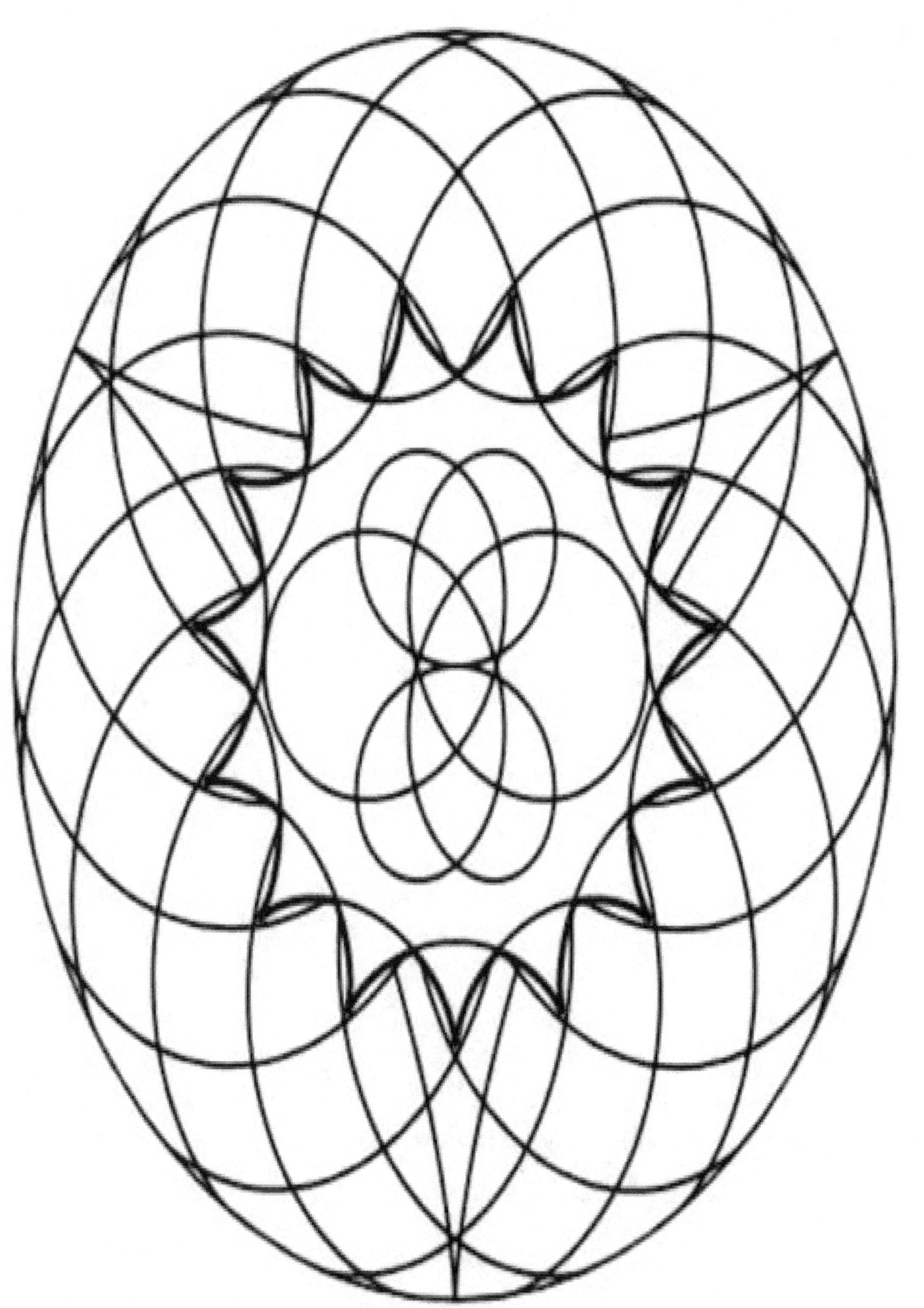

BLANK

PAGE

www.ingramcontent.com/pod-product-compliance
Lightning Source LLC
Chambersburg PA
CBHW081736220526

45468CB00008B/2125